Arthur Bl

STREET UNIVERSITY

Ventura, California U.S.A.

The foreign language publishing of all Vision House books is under the direction of GLINT. GLINT provides technical help for the adaptation, translation, and publishing of books for millions of people worldwide. For information regarding translation contact: GLINT, P.O. Box 6688, Ventura, California 93006.

STREET UNIVERSITY

Third Printing, 1984

Published by Vision House
Ventura, California 93006
Printed in U.S.A.

Library of Congress Catalog Card No. 78-60706
ISBN 0-88449-037-8

*Dedicated to the good news of Jesus
going forth to all the world.
To every person,
that all may know Jesus as Saviour and Lord.
To the glory of God.*

*And to my wife, Sherry,
and my six children,
Gina, Joel, Joy, Joshua, Joseph and Jerusalem,
who have witnessed with me in all the world,
and who have spent much time alone
as I have spent the night in the streets
helping someone find Jesus.*

CONTENTS

WITNESSING IS SERIOUS FUN

This book is written to help equip you for better sharing of Jesus Christ in the world in which you live. I am constantly asked, "How can I start telling others about Jesus? What can I do to reach my neighborhood, my street, the downtown area of my city?" Other related questions also come up such as, "How do I start an outreach ministry? How can my church evangelize the community? How can I go into a nightclub and witness? How do I know when God is leading me to go somewhere or do something?"

I tried to share in this book what my experience has been and how it relates to what the Bible says about evangelism. I have shared Christ in hundreds of nightclubs and bars around the world. I have witnessed to people of every color and of every major religion, and I have carried a cross around the world sharing the good news of Jesus with thousands of people along the way.

Furthermore, I've personally trained thousands of people in outreach evangelism during the last fifteen years. Most of these have worked with me on the streets, in bars or in other outreach projects. They have learned as they have simply shared Jesus alongside of me, without having received any formal instruction. They have absorbed the method as we have worked together. This kind of teaching, through living together day by day, is ideal, but time and opportunity are limited. As a result, I have only been able to train a small, but powerful, group every year.

I have also been involved in training seminars for youth groups or churches. I teach them for an hour or so, then send them out to talk with people in their neighborhood or their community's nightlife area. It has been thrilling to see people who have never before shared Jesus in a personal way suddenly become alive and effective in leading others to Him.

From this reservoir of experience in churches, in crusades and in personal witnessing, I pass on to you what I have learned. I trust it will be used of God to help you better share Jesus with your world.

Much of what I will be passing on to you has no direct support in the Bible. There's no Bible passage that outlines how you are to witness in a bar, or how you should approach someone at the beach, or how to go door to door in a modern apartment unit, or how you can witness at McDonald's. We can get an idea of how to do these things through studying the life of Jesus Christ, through reading the book of Acts, through studying the prophets of the Old Testament, but we need to translate evangelism in the Bible into the context and the circumstances that surround us today. So I may be talking about approaching a person at a 7-11 store or at a rock-and-roll concert, or in someone's house or at a church service. There will be a wide range of approaches, *but the purpose is always the same: to lead a person to know Jesus Christ as his personal Savior and Lord.* Regardless of where they are approached, they must understand who Jesus is and what their condition is, and that they must make a response, the positive response of receiving Jesus Christ as their Savior and Lord! That is the purpose in every one of our approaches.

I want to begin with what will be our basic Scripture passages for our witnessing motivation. It's strange, perhaps, that I have chosen two Old Testament passages, but I think you will see why they are so appropriate. The first is Psalm 40:8-10:

"I delight to do thy will, O God, yea thy law is within my

> heart. I have preached righteousness in the great congregation: lo, I have not refrained my lips, O Lord, thou knowest. I have not hid thy righteousness within my heart; I have declared thy faithfulness and thy salvation; I have not concealed thy loving kindness and thy truth from the great congregation."

How many of you can say that the righteousness of God is in your heart. Then where is God's salvation? In your heart, right. That's great, but should it stay there? No, the righteousness of God needs to be expressed with your lips. The salvation of God needs to be declared.

There are some people who say, "Well, the way I walk is my witness." Well, I defy anybody to go down Hollywood Boulevard, or Sunset Strip, look at the people walking by and tell me who's saved. You can't tell by the walk—whether they are taking long steps or little short steps, whether they are wearing blue jeans or a tuxedo—who's saved and who isn't. Unless someone *tells* you that he is saved or witnesses to you, you can't be sure whether he is born again or just self-righteous. Even if you work around someone on the job who is honest and smiles a lot and is well behaved and contributes to every charity and does everything you'd think a Christian should do, you can't be sure, because there are some people who are trying hard to work their way to heaven. They may look like others who are truly born again. Therefore, unless our lips *speak* salvation, unless our lips *declare* His righteousness, the world will not know how to be saved. Romans 10:13-15 tells us that people can't hear without a preacher:

> "For, every one who calls upon the name of the Lord will be saved. But how are men to call upon him in whom they have not believed? And how are they to believe in him of whom they have never heard? And how are they to hear without a preacher? And how can men preach unless they are sent? As it is written, 'How beautiful are the feet of those who preach good news!' "

We must, therefore, preach the Word of God.

It doesn't matter whether you are a man or a woman, God is concerned that the message is declared. He will use a woman declaring the message of Christ as effectively as He will a man. In John 4, we read about Jesus talking to a Samaritan woman. She believed and was converted, and then she dropped her water pots, ran into the city and spoke to the *men*. John doesn't record that she said a word to the women. They probably wouldn't talk to her anyway because she was so wicked. But, she spoke about Jesus to the men, and the men came out and heard Him themselves, and they had revival in that town.

The message of the resurrection was entrusted to a woman to go and tell the disciples. So we encourage both men and women to bear witness to Jesus freely. A woman can share Christ with a man or a man with a woman or they may share with people of their own sex. It doesn't matter; God's interested in *using you* for His glory and He wants to go to work through your life. You can share Jesus Christ with anybody.

Sometimes I'm so excited, I can't contain myself even when there are no people around. When I was in Africa and there were monkeys in the trees, I'd walk by and say, "Just in case you can understand me, Jesus loves you. I didn't want to miss anybody!"

Our burden is to declare His salvation to "the great congregation." Who is the congregation? The world, the *whole* world. Now, the psalm writer wasn't just talking about giving a testimony at church. Some of us find we've got plenty of enthusiasm as long as we are in the building, but as soon as we get out of the building our lips are sealed. It is easy to find people who can praise God in the auditorium, but they don't impress me unless they're witnessing out in the world. If you're only excited when you're in the building, something is wrong. Declare His righteousness and His salvation to the *great* congregation, to the *world*.

The second Bible passage for motivation in witnessing is Psalm 144:12 and 13.

> "That our sons may be as plants grown up in their youth; that our daughters may be as corner stones, polished after the similitude of a palace; that our garners may be full, affording all manner of store; that our sheep may bring forth thousands *and ten thousands in our streets.*"

Who are the sheep? *We* are the sheep. He's the Shepherd and we're the sheep. The Shepherd wants the sheep to bring forth thousands and ten thousands *in the streets.* So our thrust should be to bring those who are lost into the fold that we may reproduce ourselves by seeing people come to Jesus Christ. The "streets" of the world are wherever the wandering sheep have gone. Wherever people are, there ought to be someone telling the story of Jesus, telling them that they can be saved. Isn't that exciting?

If you let these two passages become your spiritual heartbeat, you'll notice a change in your living and your witness.

Of course, the New Testament continues this emphasis. Jesus Himself is the best example. He said: "Go into all the world and preach the gospel to every person," and He said, "Go into the highways and hedges and compel them to come in that my house may be full." Jesus Himself showed the way. He went into every city and village preaching the gospel of the Kingdom. He placed Himself in many different circumstances. We find Him going to a wedding party. We see Him being with lepers. We see Him talking to the harlots. We see Him in the Temple. We see Him in the marketplace. We see Him at the well where the people are gathering. We see Him in the public and private places of His day. Then, when we read the book of Acts, we discover that the early Christians did the same sort of thing. Sometimes Paul preached in the marketplace. Sometimes Peter was in a private home. Sometimes they were in the streets. Sometimes they were on board a ship, and wherever they were they were preaching and sharing. They expressed the gospel in every circumstance of their lives. Even when they were in prison they were preaching.

Now, this style of witnessing was not just intended for the Bible days. Study the history of the Christian Church since the time of Christ up to our present day. You'll see that throughout history missionaries have gone everywhere, even into the jungles, and have given their lives in proclaiming the Gospel of Christ. You'll read about the people who spent years in prison. You'll read about some whose heads were cut off. Yet they obeyed the thrust of the gospel to go into all the world. It is because they have obeyed Jesus' command that there are church buildings all over the globe. These are testimonies to the lives of personal witnesses. Very seldom was the building built first. Someone went in and shared Christ, and soon so many people were saved that they couldn't get them together in one place without building a special structure.

In that same spirit, *we* need to go into all the world today with the good news of Jesus Christ. I'm going to share with you a lot of stories about how this is being done today. Some of them are funny stories, and I hope you'll have a good time as you read them. I have more fun serving Jesus than anybody I've ever met. But don't let the humor cause you to forget that witnessing is *the most serious work in the world.*

God bless you as you prepare yourself to go into the "highways and hedges" of your neighborhood with the saving message of Jesus.

Your servant in Christ,
Arthur Blessitt
Luke 18:1

1
WITNESSING IN THE STREETS

1

God's Power to Change Lives

God Can Save

Effective witnessing begins with a conviction that God can change a person's life and that He *wants* to perform that miracle. He has the power and the desire to make your life new, to make anybody's life new. The Bible says, "Therefore, if any man be in Christ, he is a new creation. Old things are passed away, behold all things have become new" (2 Corinthians 5:17). We must realize that God is able to change anyone in an instant. In one moment He can save a soul and make a person new. Salvation is not necessarily a process that takes weeks or months or years. It is not necessarily a process that involves one visit after another. God is able to save anyone who comes to Him and make his life new in an instant. A person who has never heard of the Lord Jesus Christ, has never even heard the name before, can meet a witness who shares with him about Jesus and be saved through one conversation and through one prayer.

Sometimes we have to go back to see them over and over again before they give their lives to Christ. But this is not because God can't save them in one visit. It's because they've not allowed Him to do the job. However, you will not be a consistent, effective, dynamic witness for Jesus unless you allow God to fill you with His Spirit, to such a degree that you fully believe Jesus Christ can change any person right on the spot. If you don't have that confidence, then you'll not witness with the same effective power.

God Can Save Anyone

I remember when I first came down to Sunset Strip in 1967. I had a desire to try to get a lot of seminary students and pastors and strong, mature Christians to come down and witness with me. But the whole Strip at that time was full of kids who were dressed differently from the normal standard of that day. Many were loaded on drugs, freaky, spaced out. Some were loaded on downers and old Ripple wine. Soon I found that I faced a grave problem. The Christians who were coming down to witness didn't believe that God was able to change these people. Everyone they started to witness to was loaded on either uppers or downers. Some seemed too freaky to be saved, and others were into some sort of a trip from which the Christians didn't think they could be set free. So we had Christians who came down to witness, but I couldn't get them convinced that God was able to save. The problem wasn't with the lost, but with those doing the witnessing.

Then, I found that we had better success with a group of laymen who didn't have a deep basis of theological knowledge, but who did have a close walk with Jesus. We'd take them down on the street and train them and share with them how to tell people about Jesus, and they'd end up praying with people and seeing them saved. We also had good results with new converts who had lived in that scene and went back to people they'd been friendly with to tell them about the Lord. They believed that God could change lives because it had happened to them.

I have seen people who had never been into lives of degradation witnessing next to others who had been delivered. I have seen precious young girls talking to big old tough guys, telling them about Jesus Christ, with the absolute faith that God is going to save them. They *knew* Christ could change their lives. If you sent most theologians down to witness to the same people, they wouldn't be as effective. They'd start off talking about the creation or about some issue of theology, and they'd screw their minds up worse than they're already screwed up. But, little people start telling them about Jesus and in a minute they've got their heads bowed and they're praying and giving their lives to Him.

God Can Save Through Anyone

Now, God will tolerate your knowledge if you'll let it be used for His glory. But just having a lot of theological knowledge is nothing but intellectual foolishness, without the belief that Jesus is able to save all who come to Him. The Bible tells us that God has chosen the simple preaching of the gospel of Jesus Christ to save those who are lost. Paul said the preaching of Christ is to some foolishness, to others it's a stumbling block, but to those who are born again, it's the power of God unto salvation. You must believe that God is able.

I know God is able. My dad had a serious problem with alcohol, but Jesus changed him. He became new inside and out. His vocabulary changed, his behavior changed, he began to read the Bible and pray with his family. He decided that he would never go into a bar again.

I said, "Daddy, that's not right. We need to go back down there and witness for Jesus. You need to tell them that the Lord's changed you, so that they can see His power to change them." Finally, my dad gathered up our biggest family Bible, and the two of us began to witness in those same bars. He kept it up until he died years later — red hot for God.

One time I was visiting at home, and there was a new pastor at our family church. He took me aside and said to me, "Arthur, I know you go all around the world preaching, and we're proud of you here at the church where you were saved. But, I'll tell you, your dad shoots pool down at the pool hall in the afternoons. He's there almost every day. Why don't you try to talk your dad out of shooting pool down at the pool hall?" And I said, "How many people have been saved through my dad's witness down there? My dad goes down there and shoots pool and tells people about Jesus. He carries his Bible in there, and he witnesses for the Lord Jesus Christ while he's shooting pool and playing dominoes."

Now, that's not my trip, and that's not my way of witnessing on a daily basis. I don't know how in the world he could stand being around those little old rolling balls so much, but he did. And, he was down there witnessing and leading men to Jesus Christ. He wasn't talking like the rest of them, he wasn't living like the rest of them, but he was leading them to Jesus. So I said to the pastor, "Leave my daddy alone. He's in a lot better shape than he used to be. Leave him alone."

God has the power to straighten *you* out and to change *you*. I've seen people for whom there seemed to be absolutely no hope, and I've seen God change them. I could go on for hours just telling you of people that I've personally talked with who were drug addicts or prostitutes or drug dealers or businessmen or housewives, and they have been changed by Christ. He is able to make your life new. God is in the business of changing lives everywhere. "Whosoever cometh to me," He said, "I will in no wise cast out" (John 6:37).

Seeing God Change Lives is Exciting

I am happy just to be able to tell somebody how Jesus can make them new. I get the greatest thrill out of that. I get happier when somebody is saved than I do hearing that the Dodgers won a ballgame, because all the ballgames in the world will never add up to one soul's eternal destiny. I see people who get excited about ballgames and about everything else in the world except Jesus. But, I can't help it, what excites me is people being saved; I make no apologies about it. As a matter of fact, I pray to the Lord that I will become more excited every day.

When we baptize people at our center, we clap and

praise the Lord. We *ought* to jump up and down and stomp when someone's saved. When a person gets a ball over a fence, we become ecstatic. Someone kicks a ball that isn't even round over a crossbar and we think it's really outstanding. A guy hits a tiny, white ball with a club, and we become excited.

I come walking along the roads of the world with the cross. I may walk by a golf course, and there's the guy standing out there with his little old pole with a knot on the end, trying to knock a ball in a hole a couple of hundred feet away. I go by carrying a cross, and he thinks *I'm* weird. I look at him, and I think he's weird.

Then, there are others who bat a ball across a net — bat, bat, bat. It isn't over 50 or 75 feet, and they spend all afternoon hitting that ball back and forth. And they think they're normal! They holler all these weird numbers like love — 15. This is the truth. I was going through Florida, near Key West, and I walked by a tennis court. A group of Christians were with me. Some people were out there playing tennis. One guy hollered "Love — 15." I hollered, "No, not love — 15; love John 3:16." I went on into town. The next morning I was preaching at First Baptist Church of Key West, Florida. When I finished preaching, a girl rushed up. She said, "Was it you yesterday that came by the tennis court with the cross?" I said, "Yes." She said, "My brother came home from playing tennis yesterday afternoon and told me that some guy had come by dragging a big cross and had hollered, 'No, not love — 15; love John 3:16.' My brother said, 'You're a Christian; tell me what he meant.' " She told him about Jesus and prayed with him, and he gave his heart to Jesus. It doesn't take more than a little bit sometimes.

We get people excited over balls — pool balls, ping pong balls, volleyballs, handballs, baseballs, footballs, basketballs, every imaginable kind of ball. I'm thinking about making a round Bible. If we made a round Bible, you couldn't get down the street with it under your arm. Everybody would say, "Give me one, give me one." You may see some guy wearing little old briefy britches, with a big number 79 on his shirt, and you think he's out of sight. If the same guy came along with "Jesus Saves" on his T-shirt, everybody would look at him kind of funny. Right?

Some big brute may be able to run with a ball with laces and get it over a line. They try and try and try, and they hardly ever make it. If the other folks wouldn't knock them down, they'd do it in one play. But there they are, running around all bad and grisly and mean, getting all turned on because of that funny ball and yet they think they're okay.

Be Bold, Be Enthusiastic

You should make no apology for being excited that God is able to change a life. You should be bold about it. I have witnessed to nearly every presidential candidate that's run in the last two presidential campaigns. As you may know, I once entered a presidential primary. I didn't win the nomination, but I got 1½% of the votes in New Hampshire and Florida. I tell you, I saw people that were excited to death. All they could think about was Muskie, McGovern, Burch Bayh, Frank Church, Brown, Carter. If you can get turned on over that bunch of politicians, you ought to be able to get excited about the Lord. I talked to them. I met them, and I didn't see a whole lot to get excited about. With all due respect, they were still just human beings. Yet I saw people who talked constantly about their candidate, but they couldn't even mention the name of Jesus. They went out and put handbills all over the place. They'd put a presidential candidate's bumper sticker on their cars, but they wouldn't think about putting on a Jesus sticker. I can't understand the mentality of being excited about such secular things and having no excitement about the Lord. We are living and working and sharing for the one that's able to save the world. He deserves our love. He deserves our enthusiasm. He deserves and He's worthy of everything we've got.

Witnessing Is Worth the Sacrifice

I remember when I was in college. We were having compulsory chapel services, and I hated to go to them because they brought in the driest speakers they could find. One day I was sitting in the back row and I saw the speaker come in. He was an old man. I said to myself, "Oh, my, what a chapel service. If we're going to have to sit here and listen to the program, they ought to get someone who can at least walk fast. This poor old fella can hardly stand up." I was bored stiff just waiting for him to come on.

He was introduced, and he walked up very slowly. I looked around and saw that everybody had the same feeling I did. Then he began to speak. He didn't speak fast and he didn't speak loudly. But we all began to listen when he told how he was in China, how he'd been beaten, how he'd been in jail, how he had seen friends dying for the name of Jesus. My soul was stirring. He pointed his finger toward that audience and said: "God is either worthy of vour best or nothing at all. He's worth living for all the way, or He's not even worth starting with."

I sat there crying. I said, "Lord, forgive me, have mercy on me. Lord, I want to go with You all the way. I want to give You my life, every ounce of it, the best of it. Use me, use me." I want to tell the *world* about Jesus. He wants to save everyone who comes to Him, and He can do it.

Let me give you a few simple illustrations. We had moved out on Sunset Strip, but we'd been evicted from our building in 1969. I had been arrested on the streets for loitering. They wouldn't let us stand on the sidewalk. Our building had been right up above Sneaky Pete's, Whiskey-a-Go-Go and Big Al's, and they wanted us out of the neighborhood because our sign ("God is Love") was hurting business. The judge said that we were not guilty of any violation, but taken as a whole our work was out of context with the other businesses in the block. (Praise the Lord.) We had to leave. We couldn't stay on the streets or we'd be arrested. We couldn't stay in the building.

So we moved out. We carried our wooden cross out of the vacated building, tied a big old chain around the top and attached the chain to my wrist. I sat down at the foot of the cross and said I was going to fast and pray until Jesus came or until we got a new building. I knew that the Lord would help us do what He'd called us to do there. Eventually, it took 28 days of praying and preaching and fasting there on the sidewalk, right outside Sneaky Pete's on Sunset Strip. The reason I did it at first was just to keep from being arrested. They'd been simply picking me up. Well, I knew if I was chained to a cross, they'd have to come with the fire department, blow torches, everything else. It would cause such a sensation, because we were guilty of no crime. It wouldn't look good. They allowed nightclubs and everything else all around, but they wouldn't let us have a place for God.

Enthusiasm for Jesus Attracts Attention

As soon as we were out on the street, along came the news media. "Some nut chained to a cross down on Sunset Strip." One of the news reporters was sent down by his editor at the *Herald Examiner*. His name was Bob Friedman. He was Jewish. He came down with his photographer to cover this weirdo on a cross. As I always do, I witnessed to the news reporters, and so I began talking to Bob. Well, he wasn't really interested, but the next day he came back to do a follow-up. Then he started coming down every day. Once a week the paper would do an article telling how our sit-in was progressing, but Bob kept coming every day.

Finally, I told him, "Bob, I don't believe the Lord is going to let me be unchained from this cross and have a new building until you get saved. The Lord wants me right here, because if I leave, you won't be back." I started praying hard for Bob, because I really was getting tired of being on that cross. On the 27th day, Bob came and I started talking to him. I said, "Bob, give your life to Jesus." He listened to everything. We'd been through the Old Testament, the New Testament, everything. I just kept talking to him about Jesus, just Jesus, and the Spirit of God was working. Finally, I reached out my hand and said, "Bob, take my hand, let me pray with you right now, give your life to Jesus." I started praying, and then he prayed. He gave his life to Jesus Christ and got up a new man, saved, changed. He was still Jewish, in fact he was more Jewish than he had ever been. He knew the Messiah, because he had accepted Him as his Savior and Lord. You may have read Bob's little book, *What's a Good Jewish Boy Like This Doing in First Baptist Church?* He has since written other books, and he's now in Hollywood still living for Jesus. Christ *is* able to change and save.

God's Power to Save Is Worldwide

I have seen God change lives all over the world. I've seen people who have received Jesus and immediately gone out and destroyed the idols they had been worshiping. I've seen people who have given their lives to Jesus Christ and have immediately gone back to their houses and brought out all the things they'd been into — Satan-worship, black magic, etc. — and burned and destroyed them. I've seen millionaires who have been convicted by the Spirit of God and repented, then have given their hearts to Jesus and been saved. I've seen children born again, just as I was. I needed to be saved as a 7-year old boy as much as Hitler did. It doesn't take any more of the grace of God to save the worst murderer in the country than it does to save the smallest child. We all have the same need to be saved.

God is able to save and to change and to make life new. And I trust that everyone who is reading this book has found this out for himself. If you believe what God is able to do, then act on it; you will live differently. You'll witness where normally you wouldn't have witnessed. There'll be no prejudice that tells you some guy is too far gone.

Is There Anyone Who Can't Be Saved

There may be (and from the scripture I find indication that there are) some people who *cannot* be saved but the impossibility is on their side, not God's. They've hardened their hearts, they've resisted the call of the Holy Spirit of God, and they just won't listen to His voice any more. They could be saved if they'd listen, but they won't. But, only God knows who these people are. You don't and I don't. So don't ever say, "That guy's too hard. I'm not going to witness to him," or, "This person is too far gone, I won't witness to him." The only one who can judge is God, and He won't mind you witnessing if that person isn't going to be saved anyway. He wants you to tell the story. Don't prejudge people. Don't play God and say they can't be changed. Believe and carry out the commission of Christ.

Looking for God's Potential in Every Lost Person

If you let God fill you with that excitement, you will look at every person you meet in the way they *can* be, not the way they are. Every man is a prospective preacher. Every woman is a prospective witness for Jesus. My dad told me some things when I left home to go out preaching. He looked at me and he said, "Son, I want you to go now. God's called you, and I know you won't be living at home. But as you go into the world, I want you to look at every woman, whether she is the madam of a house of prostitution or the queen of England as though she was your mother, and treat her that way. I want you to look at every man, whether he is the President or a drunk in the gutter, as though he were your dad. I want you to look at every girl, no matter what her condition, as though she were your sister. And then, by the grace of God, you will never mistreat anybody, and God will use you."

So begin your witnessing to every individual with the strong faith that God can and wants to make him or her a unique and a beautiful person. That's what the miracle of salvation is all about.

2

It Can Happen in the Streets

The motivation for our witnessing is expressed in Psalm 40:8-10 and Psalm 144:12-13. In the first passage the field in which we should witness is described as "the great congregation," that is, the whole world. In the second passage we are told to witness "in our streets," right out where we rub shoulders with the lost people of our particular community. I have always taken this literally and put most of my effort into street witnessing.

Street Corner Pulpits

There are a number of different aspects of street evangelism, and I want to cover these in a somewhat systematic order. I will start with what we usually think about first when we hear of street witnessing. Most of us think of it in terms of standing on the sidewalk and preaching. Now, as a matter of practice I do very little of that on a day-by-day basis. Given an equal choice, I would rather *talk* with an individual, or with five individuals, about Jesus Christ than to *preach* to them. The only time I want to preach — you know, stand back and proclaim the Word — is when there are so many people that I can't get to them on a one-to-one basis. I find that I can lead people to Christ much faster and much more effectively by sharing with them as individuals. So that is the normal practice of my life. If I've got ten people with me and we can talk to a whole block person to person, then I'd rather not preach to the whole block, but get to them individually instead.

Now, I've found that some people are only comfortable preaching. They've got boldness, but they don't like to talk to people one-on-one. They're not afraid of crowds, but they're afraid of one person. They don't want to relate on a human basis with someone they're dealing with. So they stand back and preach *at* them, rather than talk *to* them. This involves a lot of enthusiasm and zeal, but there is no real relationship to people.

Now, there are exceptions to all of this. There may even be times you decide to preach on an empty street to draw a crowd. Sometimes there have been places I've just stood and preached to a crowd of people jammed up at a red light for about 2 or 3 minutes before they cross to the other side. Hundreds of them may be jammed there, and sometimes I'll feel that I want to stand there and preach. One of the key things in street preaching is the attitude of the person preaching. I've seen some people preaching in such a belligerent way that everybody around wants to punch them and spit on them. But I've seen others preach in a way that causes people to be interested. They've got something to say that's attractive, and the people want to hear it. Street preaching will really prove whether what you're saying is worthwhile or not. You can preach in a church and have the sorriest sermon anyone ever heard but they're not going to get up and walk out on you. They may not come back the next Sunday, but they're just too polite to make a scene. But if you start to preach on a street and don't have anything worth saying, you're not going to have a crowd. If you've got something really attractive to say, you'll draw a crowd.

Be Creative

If they're not attracted to what you're saying, it may be their fault or it may be yours. Whatever the reason, change tactics immediately. Don't worry about it. Just change tactics. Talk to them individually. The atmosphere varies from town to town and from daylight to dark. It varies depending on which street corner you're on. So if one thing you're doing isn't reaching the people effectively, don't have a hurt ego about it. Just praise the Lord. Calm down, and start talking to people one-on-one. Or, maybe you should try singing or something else.

I've preached on the streets all over the world. We started our ministry in New York in 1971 with a blitz on Times Square for three months. The police gave us permission to use Duffy Square, a little area right in the middle of Times Square. Billy Graham had to call and arrange it because they wouldn't give it to me personally. We were going to have rallies there every night just from among the thousands milling around. So I stood on the corner and started preaching, but New York passed right on by. They didn't listen to a thing I had to say. The only time there was a crowd was when the light was red. Once in a while one or two would listen for a minute and then move on. We had come all the way from California and brought half of our team to do that witnessing. There was a singing group with us, The Crimson Bridge. They had been singing all over the country, and they came down to sing in the heart of New York. But in New York there were so many weird happenings that they didn't even notice the group was singing. The people would just kind of look around and meander on. It was bad. All around us were crowds of people, but right there on that little square was an empty spot.

Finally we sat down and prayed. This was on the second night that we had been out there. We sat down in a circle under the sky and joined hands and began to pray. We just prayed and prayed for the Lord to show us what to do. We knew the people were interested, because we were talking to them on the street, but we weren't drawing them. As we sat there praying and holding hands in our little circle, about ten of us, we began to get the feeling that there were people around us. I kind of peeked, and there they were, all around us two or three deep. They were really curious. You know, if somebody's dying on the sidewalk that'll draw a crowd. If somebody's having trouble, they'll gather around. We were sitting down holding hands, and they'd never seen anything like that.

Here was our crowd, looking and listening to what we had to say. My mind was blown. We weren't preaching to them. We just had something really wonderful that we were sharing among ourselves, and they wanted to get in on it. Then I looked up, and I said, "Just a minute. Everybody quit praying." And I said, "Let me tell you what's happening." And I started sharing a little about Jesus Christ, explaining the gospel message while we were still sitting down. I asked those that wanted to give their lives to Jesus to raise their hands so that one of us in the circle could come and talk to them. A number of people raised their hands. We went over, dealt with them and prayed with them.

Do you know that for three months we had that whole square packed for two to three services a night. There was no room to stand on that corner. Each night we'd come down around ten, and we'd sit down in our circle and we'd join hands and pray, and then the crowd would come. We had them sitting down too, then we'd start singing. We didn't even care whether New York was there. We were having a good time, and that's what was attractive. And then we'd have different ones testify, and I'd bring a short message. I couldn't preach long, because they'd only be there five minutes or so. I would give an invitation and ask the people to come up, or, if they were at the back, to raise their hands. Our workers would go back and pray with them. We'd dismiss for about 20 minutes, and then do it over again. But in order to draw the crowd we'd always have to start sitting down. If we were standing up, the crowd would scatter away. They'd seen people standing around preaching many times before. I've never used that exact strategy any place else in the world, but it worked there.

Make the Method Fit the Place

At Hollywood Boulevard and Western (called "porno corner") a different approach has worked. We witness and share with heavy drunks and people who are really into drugs. We sit down at a little El Taco place and we start singing. We take request numbers from the drunks. We say, "What would you like us to sing. Would you like us to sing a gospel song? What do you know, what song?" And they ask for "The Old Rugged Cross" or some other old favorite. This draws people from a block away. Then, when we stop singing each of us turns to someone and starts talking. Before long we're all talking to people. You have to adapt to every situation, every circumstance.

In most countries it is impossible to give out tracts, not because of the law, but because the crowds will mob you. It's unsafe. You cannot just walk out on a street in Lagos, Nigeria, and give out tracts, because within three minutes there will be hundreds of people around you, and you'll be on the floor with people trying to grab the tracts out of your hand. I've had people working with me who started to give out stickers from a roll. But the crowd was pushing and grabbing so much that they finally had to throw the roll in the air in the opposite direction and let the people run and fight. They want literature. It's a different scene.

I don't get hooked on numbers and statistics reports, but overseas I've preached to thousands of people every day. Sometimes the missionary says, "There are 20,000 people out here," or "It looks like a crowd of 75,000." I am faced with a sea of people for one or two blocks. They're jammed together, eager to hear. There is no way to counsel them, no way to deal with them personally. In situations like that I do street preaching all the time, day after day, hour after hour. I walk into any town, and the crowds gather around and I start talking.

But most of us don't have that problem. We're dealing with America where people don't gather so quickly. One of the most effective places for street preaching in small towns is the central shopping area where the kids are hanging out. There may be an ice cream stand or a little drive-in where teenagers go to pet and party. If you can find an adjoining building where you can put up a loud speaker (with permission) you can have a brief bit of good music. All the teen-age beer drinkers will come over and you can share the message of Jesus Christ and do some good personal witnessing. I find it's always better to have people working the edge of the crowd, rather than just depending on the music and the preaching to draw them. They should always work the back, because that's where people hang around when they're beginning to get interested. You can cover the teenagers from 30 miles around such a small town, and they'll keep coming back.

Saturation Witnessing

In other situations, you might use what I call saturation witnessing. That is where you cover a whole street with personal witnessing. Right at the focal point of a town or city — where the action is — assign one or two Christians to each street corner for several blocks. Then everybody who comes by there runs into someone who lovingly shares Jesus Christ with him. On his way down the block, he is hit over and over again, first on this corner, then on that corner. Some nights you can't even move on Hollywood Boulevard because of the crowds. When we do saturation witnessing there, Christians find they are approached by other Christians over and over again. Nobody minds. They just encourage each other.

One morning about three o'clock, I went into an old, dingy kind of hotel down on Western, walked in and turned to a big, tall guy who was standing there and gave him a gospel sticker. I asked, "Are you saved?" He said, "I already got one of those. I got saved tonight." I asked, "What do you mean, got saved?" He said, "I got saved on Hollywood Boulevard about midnight. Some girl came up to me and told me about Jesus, and I asked Him to come into my heart. I got saved." He just kept repeating those words.

Hitting an area on a regular, consistent basis is one of the keys to reaching that neighborhood for Christ. People get to know that every Saturday afternoon you're going to be out there on the street. It'll begin to haunt them. Every time they come into town they'll think, "There are those Christians again. They've witnessed to me every time I've come by. How do I go around the block?" If you're there every Saturday, you'll make your town aware of the witness of Jesus. If you come only once in a while, they will dismiss you. It's *consistency* that makes street ministry effective. A lot of people get excited, and they're ready to go hot and heavy for three months. But then they taper off and don't show up any more. You can be a mighty witness just by being consistent day by day, moment by moment, hour by hour. If you keep sharing Christ, sooner or later you'll be winning people to Jesus. One day you may not pray with anybody, and then the next day you may pray with ten. You may go for six hours on the streets and find hardly anybody willing to talk to you, and then in the last hour people will be standing all around you.

Your consistency in doing what God's told you to do will ultimately bring results. Someone else may be a better preacher, or a better singer, or a more effective personal witness. But if God tells you to do something, do it. If God tells you this church is your parish, then you pastor this church. Don't run around preaching all over the world. Stay in your community. If God burdens you for a certain street in a certain city, this is your place. Cancel everything else and do that job. Since the Lord has called me to carry the cross and to walk with it during a period of time, there's nothing else I'd do. When God said go to Washington, D.C., we set out on foot and made it. If somebody asked me to preach over here, to do this, to do that, I said, "No, God called me to do what I'm doing. I know what God's leading me to do now. I'm sorry, my mind's fixed on what I'm called to do." If you don't discipline yourself in this way, then you'll run over here and do this, you'll run over there and do that, and in the end you'll accomplish nothing.

Christians Can Destroy Your Ministry

As soon as you begin to be effective, you have to be careful that the demands of Christians don't destroy your ministry. The problem will not be with the lost, but with the Christians. They will destroy your street ministry more effectively than the devil can. Here's how this works. As long as you're unknown and anonymous, you can minister. But if you make it in the local town paper, or if the word spreads among Christians that your ministry is really working, then every Christian in the area wants to talk to you and every preacher in town wants you to come to his church because you'll draw a little crowd. From then on, you'll be going everywhere telling people what you *did* instead of *doing* it. You'll be actually doing nothing. You'll be a has-been reminiscing about past victories. Your street will dry up and your ministry will wither away. The world is full of has-been overnight sensations for God.

I remember what I was told years ago by Dr. Wayne Dehone, who was twice president of the Southern Baptist Convention. I was working on the Strip and some good things had happened. We'd been on television across the country. I responded to an invitation to go to Louisville. I was supposed to preach for three days in a local church but things exploded and we moved to the city auditorium. Finally we held a meeting in Freedom Hall with over 20,000 young people in attendance. After that series, I was inundated with requests from city after city to hold crusades. They wanted the same thing to happen in their city that had happened in Louisville. But Wayne said, "Arthur, let me warn you. You can go and preach at all these city-wide crusades. But what is God calling you to do? That's what you should be doing. If you let them, the Christians will destroy you. Preachers like me will ruin your ministry. We'll book you up seven days a week, and then, once you've made the circuit and everybody's heard you and you haven't *done* anything for a year, they won't want you back. It'll all be over. People will say, 'There was a guy out in Hollywood years ago. I remember that something happened out there.' Just be faithful in doing what God has called you to do. And all your life you'll have more places to preach than you can handle."

I've got to do what God's called me to do with all my heart, soul, strength and mind, and you should do what God has led you to do, consistently, day by day, year by year. There's no limit to what God will do with you if you are faithful to His call. But if you flit around from one thing to another you'll accomplish nothing.

Sensationalism: Good PR Or Just a Gimmick?

Another pitfall that comes with success in your ministry is the tendency to emphasize sensational things. This is very hard to talk about because I do many things that are looked upon as sensational. Other people try to do the same kinds of things and hope that they will get the same results. They think, "If I can use some kind of gimmick, I'll reach the city instantly." And if we don't watch it, some of us get addicted to the sensational. We sit around and think about what will draw the news media, what we can do that will get publicity. Once you start thinking that way, you're on the wrong track. Instead you should think about what needs to be done and do it. If you do it well enough and long enough, God may cause some publicity to come your way. It will come because you are consistently effective. Otherwise, it will just be a gimmick.

Some people have heard the story about our battle on Sunset Strip when I chained myself to a cross. They fail to understand the conflict we were in, the arrest we'd gone through, the closing down of our building. They do not understand the necessity we faced of having to do something vital to keep from being driven out. This was a once-in-a-lifetime situation. But they get to thinking, "Well, if I chain myself to a cross, that's all I need to do and I'll have the gospel preached all over the world." They are surprised to discover that all the news media are turned off to them. What was a dramatic witness for us has turned into a gimmick for them.

You May Get More Publicity Than You've Bargained For

If you're effective, the attention may come. But then again, it may not. Don't worry about it, because some of the greatest ministries in the world are unknown. I don't understand why it is that God chose to put me in the news media, but He did. He spoke to me one night in Tempe, Arizona, while I was walking down the street in the middle of the night praying. God burdened me so heavily that I laid down on the sidewalk and cried. God said, "I'm going to put you in the newspapers and on television, and I want you to witness to every man or woman who interviews you. You'll be my spokesman. I've called you to speak to the secular media of the world. The secular media, not the Christian media. You will preach for free to the world. Don't buy the time; go free." I couldn't conceive of the possibility that this would become a reality.

But, the next night I was preaching at Scottsdale Road Baptist Church, and after the service I got together a group of young people. We went down to a nightclub called the Fifth Estate with a big coffin we had made. We put it in front of the Fifth Estate, near the university, and we made *God is Dead* signs. When the club let out at 11:00 P.M., we were chanting "God is Dead." Then we put those signs down and put up others that said *Hallelujah He's Alive.* We took off the banner on the coffin that said *God is Dead* and under it was one that said *Jesus is Alive.* A crowd of about

1,000 people had come out of the club and were gathered around. They really got upset. They pounced on that truck and tore the coffin up. It was made out of 2 x 2s. I've learned since then not to make anything out of wood because they ripped those 2 x 2s apart, knocked me down and worked me over. The police dashed up and pulled people off me. They called a tactical alert and had to bring in the Phoenix police. The girls from our group, about 15 of them, crawled up on the truck and stood around me so that the bottles the crowd threw would hit them rather than me. At this point, the news reporters came, and the next day I was in the Phoenix newspaper and on all the television stations. I had never been on T.V. before. You see, God did what He said He would. He used a riot to do it.

The next time I preached was in San Bernardino, California, at a topless nightclub called Sinners-A-Go-Go. When I was in Phoenix, a reporter from the *L.A. Times* had asked, "Are you going to do this again?" I said, "Yeah, I'm going to be preaching at Sinners-A-Go-Go in San Bernardino." Normally, an L.A. newspaper wouldn't care about San Bernardino, but the *L.A. Times* was there because they thought another riot might break out. Then Joe Pine, who had a popular television program in L.A., saw this old freako preacher who worked in go-go clubs. He sounded like he would make a good guest. And things just went on and on. But it was *God* who did it. I didn't decide to pull a stunt to get news coverage started. God said, "I want it to be done." And, it was done.

Your Attitude Can Make the Difference

The most important aspect of street witnessing is talking person to person. You need to have a good attitude if you are going to convey the message of Christ on the street. You've got to have a sense of humor. If you can't laugh, you won't survive long. They'll get to you and destroy you. If someone is acting or talking in a crazy way, laugh at him. If you feel it's funny, laugh. You'll find that if you laugh, they'll laugh, and you'll be able to punch in the gospel in that relaxed atmosphere.

One night I came around a corner laughing. People came up and asked what I was laughing about. I said, "A guy three floors up looked out his apartment window in the middle of the night, and I yelled up to him and lead him to Jesus. Now I've got a crick in my neck, and I think that's funny." I think that's the most beautiful thing. I wasn't laughing at him but it was a funny scene being out on the sidewalk sharing the way of salvation with a guy three floors up, and saving him. I stuck the follow-up booklet and a tract and a card in the bushes so that he could come down later on and get his follow-up material.

You've got to be able to laugh. If someone is putting you down verbally, and you just ease off with a little humor, the whole atmosphere may change. You're hurting, but you grin. Anyway, that may break down a guy's defenses.

A good, happy, peaceful, tranquil attitude can change the mood in a whole area. If you're there regularly enough, you'll change it. You'll be putting out good feelings, you'll be pouring love all over the place, and the people will be attracted to it. This kind of love attracts people on a person-to-person basis.

Keep Track of Your Group in the Streets

One of the values of using tracts and stickers is that there is a way for people in the group to remember that you're all connected together. It is very important when you're taking a group out to outline where they're going and to keep them in that identifiable area. If you have a group of young people, and you load them up with tracts and turn them out on the streets but you don't tell them where to go, they will wander around town and get lost. Pretty soon it will be 11:00 or midnight and you won't know where to find them. Parents will start calling and you'll be driving all over town. Before long there won't be any Christian groups coming around because everybody's always getting lost.

When you take a group out, divide them up under strong leaders. Then give them directions, preferably to a very open area, and let them start witnessing. Set an hour when they will come together again. Make sure they meet there, even if they've got to interrupt a conversation or bring the person they're talking to along. They must be back on time or you won't be able to maintain a consistent outreach program. Your long range success depends on this. If you train people well then they'll function well. If you don't then you'll create all kinds of problems for the future.

Christians Go to the Strangest Places

The average person that you're training probably shouldn't go into places like bars and clubs. They don't need to work the dark alleys or the back streets. But *you* do. If you are committed to this kind of ministry, you need to be willing to go to anybody, anywhere, anytime. I once jokingly said that I wanted to be a street sweeper for Jesus and that's not far from the truth. If you look down a dark alley and see a bunch of hoods, you'd better make a dash right down that alley and talk to them about Jesus Christ. Keep your Bible out so they'll know who you are and what you're doing. If you're not committed to go into the worst and toughest places, then you won't be really free to witness anywhere in street ministries. I've come to the place where I do this: if there's a place in town people warn me about — "Boy, don't go there, they'll kill you" — that's the first place I go. I want to start with the worst and then it's easy from there on. If anybody ever says, "If you come back down here tomorrow night, we're going to kill you," then you can be sure I'll be there tomorrow night, because if I don't I'll let fear win. Then I'll start out, and I'll see that street every night and I'll be afraid. In time fear will run me off the streets. If you let yourself be intimidated once, it will sooner or later destroy you. It's the same when I carry the cross. If somebody says, "Don't go through this town; don't go through this country," that's where I'm going to go. I won't walk around that town, but right through it, and then I never have to worry about it. I'm not dealing with fear; I'm dealing with obedience to God's call.

For those who are called into street ministries, the greatest enjoyment and freedom come when you walk out on the street spontaneously, unstructured by time or commitments. You may be out there at seven in the evening, not worried about anything, when some people come up and say, "Hey, why don't you come to our party?" You say, "Well, I'm a preacher," and they say, "Come to the party anyway. There are about 50 of us getting together right over here at this house." What an opportunity! If I get an opening like that, I go.

Or sometimes — especially in foreign countries — a guy may come up and say, "Hey, you want to meet some nice girls, beautiful girls?" You know, prostitutes. I say, "Yeah, yeah." "Look, we've got a house of prostitution right down the street here." "Great, let's go." I don't witness on the way though. I've got my Bible in my hand. I want to get into the house before I start witnessing. And when I get there, they'll bring out a girl and say, "Do you like her?" I say, "Well, have you got any more? More? Is this all of them? Bring them all in, and let me look them over." And they bring them all in and line them up. I say, "How many of you know English?" They think I want a girl who speaks English. Maybe half of them will raise their hands. I say, "I want all of you to give your hearts to Jesus. Jesus died for your sins." I'm absolutely alone, but that doesn't matter. I'll witness and share and trust God to take care of me.

If I arrive in a strange city and I'm just going to be there one or two nights, I may go down to a corner and just stand around. I don't know what it is, but people are always offering me dope and stuff like that. I must look like a sinner or something. I just ease around and ask some guy, "Hey there, what's happening in town?" He says, "Are you just new here?" I say, "Yeah, just got in today and I leave in two days. Where's the action?" And he tells me, "You can get dope down at so and so's, if you want chicks, stay down here, and so forth. After a little bit of conversation I say, "Hey, I'm a preacher, and I want to share with you about Jesus." He asks, "Why did you want all that information?" I tell him, "Because I want to go where the sin is." Sometimes a guy like this will say, "There's a real heavy spot in town, but you've got to know somebody to get in." I say, "Well, can you get me in?" "Yeah, yeah, I can get you in." And we go to that place, and I pull out my Bible and go to work.

You Can't Let Sex Scare You Off

Working with the opposite sex presents problems for some people. I often like to work a bar at night, and I may have been witnessing to a waitress when closing time comes. Finally, I ease up and say, "Listen, it's about closing time. Can I buy you breakfast?" To me, sex doesn't enter into it. It doesn't matter whether I'm talking to a guy or a girl. I couldn't care less whether the person is a prostitute or a movie star or a drunk. You have to operate differently if you're a pastor always working in the same community. You can't go over and stay all night with one of the church members when her husband's gone. You're in a different circumstance. But when you're on the street, you've got to forget about how things work in other places and minister to the people you're working with. The daughter of the Dean of Theology at one of the most outstanding universities in this country was working on Sunset as a stripper. Long before I knew who she was, I was leading her in Bible studies in her backstage room between acts. Finally, she got right with God. When I preached at a Hell's Angels funeral, she sang "Amazing Grace." She finally called her dad and told him what had happened, and he flew out to pick her up. He didn't want to come down to Hollywood where she had been working. She said, "No, you come down here, Dad; I'm not going home until you come down and spend one night with Arthur Blessitt." And, he came down. He told me, "I don't believe in going into all these places. I don't believe it's the right thing; you shouldn't subject yourself to this kind of temptation." I asked him, "Where was your daughter reached? It's hard to tell it to you, but she didn't have her clothes on, dancing right here in this club. And I sat backstage with her while she wore only her little see-through shawl, teaching her the Bible between dances, night after night after night." I wanted him to see the scum of this world and become involved in doing something about it. He's totally different now. The girl's in full-time Christian work today. But if I hadn't gone into that club she wouldn't have been reached.

When you're involved in an outreach ministry, there are a lot of times when you jeopardize your reputation. You can't prove what you didn't do. But if you get worried about it, then you can't be an effective street minister. In time, it will destroy you. Soon, you won't be able to relate, because you've got to work with the people that are ready, wherever they are. Sometimes they don't want anybody else involved. You've got to be able to talk to them yourself alone.

Now, there are a lot of Christian women that I wouldn't drive three blocks with, because they worry me. You have to sense whether you ought to be alone with a particular person or not. But I wouldn't hesitate to drive to Las Vegas with the biggest madam in Nevada if I have a clear conscience and I'm trying to witness to her or her kids or the girls who work for her. This is a personal decision everyone has to make for himself, but that's how I operate in my life. Billy Graham has a different situation. I've been with him several times. There are always people around him. They've got to watch over him because some girl may start saying, "I spent the night with Billy Graham." They've got to be able to prove he didn't spend the night with her, keep down the rumors. But when you're involved in a street ministry, you can't protect yourself from rumors, you can't cover the corners. You've either got to accept the risk, or you can't go out there and minister.

Can You Keep a Secret?

Of course, when you're talking with people on the street, you hear a lot about the details of their lives, and you've got to learn to keep confidences. If somebody tells you something, don't go around repeating it. You might say, "Hey, I prayed with so and so," or maybe, "I was witnessing to so and so," but unless it is vital to the intimate group you're working with, don't betray their confidence. Don't tell a bunch of friends, "I witnessed to so and so and she's pregnant." She's pregnant out of wedlock, and you have started spreading the thing around. Then someone tells her, "Oh, I hear you're pregnant." Of course, the girl's hurt because you have no business repeating the personal things in people's lives.

If you run off at the mouth, you're not going to have many friends coming to you with their needs. They just can't have confidence in you. One of your best assets in any kind of ministry is the fact that people feel they can come to you and trust you. They may share the biggest scandal you've ever heard of, but let God straighten it out. Even if it's not made right, keep it all to yourself.

When You're Asked for a Handout

When you're on the streets, you're constantly faced with problems about money. Shall I give him a dollar? What about a place to stay? How about taking him home with me? These are some of the greatest agonies that I face in my life, and I don't know the answer to them all. But if I see somebody hungry, and I've got one penny in my pocket, I have to feed him. If you don't have bread at home, you can fast for 40 days. So don't worry about it if you've got to skip a meal or two or three or four. But if you've got the money in your pocket, and somebody's hungry, feed him.

That doesn't mean you should give him cash. God will have to lead me specifically for me to give someone cash, but I don't have to feel a specific leading to know I should feed a person. I may not be able to give him a T-bone steak, but if he's hungry, I'll buy him a hamburger or something. I generally won't buy a person a cup of coffee. If he's hungry and wants a cup of coffee, I say, "You need something more enriching than coffee; I'll buy you a glass of milk." If all they need is coffee, they're not really hungry. But if they're hungry, feed them.

Then, what about a place to stay? The streets are very cruel. We always find more people who need a place to stay than we have room for. There are so many in Hollywood who need a place to stay, and we just don't have the facilities. We have to tell them that. We did have a halfway house for those who had been converted and wanted to spend a month for follow up, but if that wasn't their commitment, we couldn't provide overnight lodging. I don't know any place in the Hollywood area where a person can just walk in and spend the night. It's a great temptation to take them all home. Many years ago, I used to take them all home. We had people sleeping body to body. But in my present ministry that's impossible. If you feel that God is leading you, there can be a tremendous ministry in taking people into your home and helping them right there in your own house. But this has to be done with careful discipline. You've got to make them get up and do some chores. And then send them out; don't let them hang around your house all day. Make them go out and look for a job or put them to work at your place, but don't just let them be lazy at your expense. That wouldn't be helping them.

It's a Jungle Out There

The possibility of violence is always with you when you're working on the street. You will seldom be attacked for witnessing if you use your head and are sensitive to the other person. If you realize that someone is getting uptight and mad, pleasantly say, "God bless you," and leave. And if they want to follow you along just keep saying, while walking, "God bless you," until you're out of the way.

Now, I do get into trouble. I can't help it; it's just me. I'm not recommending you do this, but if I'm on the street, and I see someone being beaten up, I get involved. I try to stop it. And I'm still alive. I may be killed doing that someday, but it's what I personally have to do. You don't have to take the same approach. I cannot pass by an auto wreck without stopping. I cannot see someone pounding another person to death and not go over, stand in-between them with my Bible and try to stop them. If you follow my approach, you'd better be sensitive and alert. Watch to see if somebody's got a chain or a knife. Make sure that you aren't mistaken for the enemy on one side or the other. Identify yourself. Say, "I'm a preacher." Even if you're not ordained say it anyway. They can understand that. Then they won't think you're taking the other guy's side. "I'm a preacher, I'm a preacher. C'mon, let's cool it. C'mon, c'mon get off the guy." But keep your Bible right out there so that everybody remembers that you are a preacher. Keep saying it, and then start sharing Jesus. If you don't, you may wind up dead, because these rumbles are bad.

If someone attacks you and you can't avoid it, then I recommend you get down on your knees and start praying. In that position your head and most other vital parts are protected. The only things that are vulnerable are your back and your kidneys, but most people won't attack you from the rear. They keep trying to kick you in the face, but with your head down and your hands over your temples and ears, you're protected pretty well. Keep your Bible between your legs. Then there's hardly any way they can get to you unless they really want to do you in, and then they're going to do it anyway.

In most situations, they'll kick for a while and then they'll quit. Hardly anyone wants to kill a person who won't fight, because it's hard to go around to your friends and brag, "I beat the tar out of that preacher." "Well, what was he doing?" "Kind of just laying there." That doesn't do anything for a guy's ego. When I'm in this kind of violent situation, I pray out loud and the harder they come, the louder I pray. But it doesn't come to that point often, because they usually back off earlier. Keep your head and you'll make the right choice for every situation. One time some guys pulled a knife on me and were going to cut my throat. I said, "God's in me, and the devil's in you. The God in me's bigger than the devil in you." But they kept coming, and in my mind I thought they were really going to do me in. I don't know whether they would have or not. All of a sudden, I took the two men by the shoulder, stepped between them, and I said, "Jesus loves you." Then I ran as fast as I could. That is the only time I have ever run in my life, but I thought it was the right thing for that situation. They were so out of it that it was time for me to move and that's what I did — fast.

Is the Law Your Friend or Enemy?

If you're going to work on the street, you need to consider what the law is as it relates to street witnessing. It is important as a practice to obey the law, to do whatever the police say. But having said that, I must also tell you that in many places the law is enforced wrongly. Also, sometimes the local laws are unconstitutional. Therefore, if you're beginning a permanent ministry, it may be necessary to file some kind of legal suit. You may even have to be arrested.

Let me give you an example. I was invited by the ministers in Daytona Beach, Florida, to come down for the week of the motorcycle races. We had arranged for the band shell even though the city of Daytona Beach has an ordinance against our kind of public religious meetings. They require you to have a permit to pass out materials. Then if a group like ours comes in they use this ordinance to run them out of town. There was no question in our minds that the law was unconstitutional, so we ignored it. We had churches and other groups involved so we decided to make a stand as a matter of principle. We invited the police to come to one of our sessions, and the captain got up and told us that we would be arrested for giving out the material because of this ordinance. We said, "Well, you'd better be ready. We're all going to start passing out material at 3:00 this afternoon, all these pastors and everybody else. You'd better have all your squad cars handy." The preachers had some lawyers who were ready to go to court. We felt we couldn't concede their control over the passing out of tracts. It would have been overruled in court instantly. Now, when the police realized we were actually going to do it, they backed off. They refused to enforce the ordinance for a week, so that it would still be on the books. They decided to let us get away with it because of our size and power, but the next little old lonely Christian that came out and started passing out tracts would be run out of town.

So if you're going to establish a continuing street ministry, you need to be aware of what the laws say and what your rights and liberties are. As a general practice, obey and cooperate with the police, but many times they're wrong and need to be confronted. We have loitering laws and disturbing the peace laws that have been passed by local governments and are vague and unconstitutional. Then police officers are given liberty to stretch the law and misuse it to deny people their rights. When that is happening, you initially need to back off until you get the thing straight and clear.

Don't ever be arrested for something that is against a constitutional law and can lead to a conviction. For instance, when you're in a shopping center, you have to leave if you're asked. That's private property. Don't block a business doorway. If you are witnessing, stay away from the door, stand at a good reasonable distance. You can reach everyone going and coming even if you are at a fairly reasonable distance and then they can't say that you're blocking their business. We wouldn't want people blocking the entrance to our church, and we should be considerate of these businessmen.

Sometimes a street minister will have a confrontation with a certain police officer, and the thing becomes a continuing feud. There are good police officers and there are sometimes bad ones just as there are good preachers and bad ones. But don't ever start a running war of hatred with an unreasonable policeman. Don't ever let it become personal with the guy.

If you are taken to court, remember that you have a right to a lawyer. It's a guarantee of our Constitution. They must assign you legal counsel if you can't afford your own. He's called the Public Defender. I have found that in almost every case the Public Defender is really on the side of the person being prosecuted. Although he is provided by the government, he is not defending the government. He is a regularly trained attorney and his legal mind is just as good as those of other lawyers. However, many of them are overloaded with a hard case load. So they may not have enough time to give your case the best treatment. The American Civil Liberties Union may seem like a dirty word to a lot of Christians, but let me tell you, they will defend you if it involves a constitutional matter. They've taken cases for me in the past when they have involved constitutional issues. Hardly any of them are Christians, but they are wonderful, totally committed, dedicated. I can't say enough for the lawyers that I've been involved with in the ACLU. But you have to begin by presenting your case to the ACLU and proving to them that it involves constitutional matters. It's true they fight for keeping prayer out of schools, but they'll also fight for your right to speak on the street.

If You Have Knowledge of a Crime

When you're working in the streets, you may come upon knowledge about crimes and not know what to do about it. To me, this is a very tricky subject. I draw a fine line in my life. If someone is being beaten up, or if I see a bank robbery in progress, or something like that, as an individual citizen, I don't hesitate to call the police. If a public crime is taking place, it needs to be stopped. I would feel free to call the police because I don't want innocent people to be hurt.

On the other hand, if I'm talking with somebody and he says, "I need help," and then he opens up to me and tells me that he's robbed a bank or killed somebody or that he's wanted by the F.B.I., that's a different situation. This has been told in the context of a counseling situation. As a rule, I do not turn people in when they have confided in me. It would totally close the opportunities of reaching street people. I view it as a minister, a counselor; I am like a priest taking confession. Now, I always try to get such a person to go back and face his problem. My counsel is always that they turn themselves in. I have taken many people that I've prayed with, shared with, dealt with and I've gone with them to the police station while they've turned themselves in. But I don't turn them in.

I remember one guy who came into my building on Sunset Strip one night. He listened to the message and then he called me upstairs to the prayer room and said, "I've got to talk. Are you for real?" I said, "I'm for real." He said, "Are you really?" I said, "Yes." He said, "I'll tell you, I'll kill you if you betray my confidence. Someday I'll get out of jail, and I'll hunt you down and kill you, but I've got to talk." I said, "Don't worry about it, brother; talk to me."

And we talked and shared, hour after hour. I prayed with him. He was wanted for all sorts of things. But he gave his life to Jesus Christ. He asked, "What do I do now?" I counseled with him and he decided to turn himself in. We went down to the West Hollywood sheriff's station, where he tried to surrender but nobody would take him at first. No, you just can't go down to jail and be booked. "Sit out here and wait a while." Well, we sat out there for about an hour while they checked with the F.B.I. Then about seven officers came in with their hands on their guns. They slapped handcuffs on him. I said, "Hey, fellas, don't handcuff him, let him at least walk into the station. Just this last breath of freedom." But, Whamo! In he went. He was sent down to the Florida penitentiary and we had him enrolled in a Bible correspondence course. And, he went on spiritually. He stayed in prison three years instead of the thirty years he thought he would have to spend. Now he's married, has a family and is pastor of a church.

During the Vietnam War, we were always dealing with guys who were runaways from the service. And we always tried to get them to go back to their base and face up to the situation. I still believe that's the best course of action for anyone in trouble. But the person has to make the decision himself. He has to be able to confide in you. That's the only way you get to reach people of the street. I've had people confess to all sorts of things. And I've had approaches from different state and federal agencies about people I know and what they've done. But I just won't talk about it. "I'm sorry, I've nothing to say." I can't because it would destroy a ministry that I have with a lot of people. You may think you can break these confidences and get by with it, but somewhere the street people have a listening ear, and the word will come back. "You squealed on so-and-so." And your ministry will be dead. But if you are trustworthy, more and more people will confide in you and they'll find a way to get you when they need help. And, they'll know that's the end of it — period!

Should Baby Christians Witness?

I am often asked if new converts should witness on the streets. My answer is yes. Even if you hardly know the Bible, go out and share anyway. Share what you *do* know. Of course, you shouldn't neglect Bible study; you should be studying the Word all the time. But if you wait to start witnessing until you know everything there is to know, you'll never begin.

There's one church in Mississippi that is widely known for its great evangelistic ministry. People are always finding Christ through its influence. I asked the pastor one time: "How come you're winning so many of these atheists and agnostics. Over and over, I hear people testifying, 'I used to be an atheist.' " And he said to me, "Well, Arthur, when we get in touch with someone who says he's an atheist, I never send my deacons, I never send our mature Christians to witness to them. I send two of our newest converts." I asked, "Why do you do that?" He said, "Because these new converts don't know enough about the Bible to even discuss it intelligently. They just got saved. They'll come in and sit down and start talking to that person. He may say, 'There's nothing to the blood of Jesus, the Bible's not the Word of God,' and all that intellectual stuff. These two new converts can't answer him at all. They're pushed back in a corner. Finally, they'll just start crying and say, 'I don't know all this stuff you're telling me, but I know I got saved last week, and Jesus came into my heart and I'm born again, and He loves you. They'll just start crying and praying. They win people to the Lord because they're for real. Through them they see that Jesus is alive."

Now, you need more of a testimony than that through the years. If you try to live off your new convert testimony, pretty soon it will be stale and won't work. But when you have a new convert, put him out there and let him go. Get him started instantly.

Should Baby Christians Witness?

I am often asked if new converts should witness on the [illegible] [illegible] [illegible] [illegible] [illegible] [illegible] Of course [illegible] [illegible] [illegible] [illegible] [illegible] [illegible] [illegible] [illegible] [illegible] [illegible] something [illegible] [illegible] [illegible] [illegible]

[illegible] [illegible]

[illegible] [illegible] [illegible] [illegible] [illegible] [illegible] [illegible] [illegible] [illegible] [illegible] [illegible] [illegible]

3
It Can Happen in Night Spots

A Neglected Area of Witness

I understand that not everyone has been called to minister in bars and nightclubs, but I want to share this information with all of you so you will realize that God can work anywhere. I will explain how to get started and be effective at such a ministry and also how you can establish a continuing, permanent ministry to the night spots of your community. Then you will have to decide whether or not this kind of witnessing is something to which God is calling you.

Bars, nightclubs and other scenes of nightlife in our cities make up one of the most neglected mission fields in the world. Yet, this kind of ministry doesn't fit into any normal pattern of Christian ministry. This is because of the way the Christian culture operates. The usual idea is that ministry is done from nine to five. That's when church offices are open. The only other time when Christians function in ministry would be from about seven to about nine in the evening, and then they are usually closed up in their buildings. But outside of those normal functioning times and places, the witness of Christianity is generally silent.

Almost all of the streets of the world are void of a consistent witness for Jesus. Almost all of the night scenes are void of any consistent witness. You might take a map of the U.S., close your eyes, point at a town and say you will begin a ministry there. I don't know of one place that's overcrowded with too much street ministry of the right sort. I don't know of any city that has too many people sharing Jesus on a consistent basis. And this is especially true in the area of night life.

Don't Be Afraid of Night People

A nightlife ministry seems scary to most people. We have the idea that people in bars, nightclubs, pornographic bookstores and other businesses that operate at night wouldn't be interested in Christians coming around. We have the idea that this would be the hardest group of people to reach. We expect that these would be the meanest people; they would want to kill you, knock you down, stomp you, drag you out. But I want you to know that you'll never be around any group of people that are friendlier and warmer (except for a close, beautiful fellowship of spiritual Christians) than you'll find around most of the bars and nightclubs. If they weren't friendly people, they wouldn't be there. They are generally lonely people looking for companionship. The person who is comfortable with his life can stay home and watch television all night. But the person who is really lonely, or who has a lot of energy and doesn't know what to do with it, the person who can't cope with himself . . . he is the one who is out in the middle of the night.

And you can almost chart this: the later in the night it is, the higher is the percentage of people who will pray with you for salvation. The later in the night it is, the lonelier the people are and the more they realize their emptiness and their need for Jesus Christ.

Most people in these clubs are the same as the people you work with on the job in the daytime. You don't have to be afraid of them because they are like your next door neighbor. You may have an idea built into your mind that there is a bunch of wild people who hang out in such places, and you wouldn't know how to talk to them if you ever met them. But they are really much like the people you deal with at work or in your neighborhood. By day, they are average, normal people. At night they are lonely and hungry for friendship. There is no reason to be terrorized thinking that there are monsters in a night spot anymore than you are terrorized by the people you work with.

Let me share something else with you. I don't think most men go out into bars to try to find a woman to spend the night with. I don't think most women go in just to find someone to come to their house. I think most people simply want someone to visit with. They just want to talk to a person; they're hungry for fellowship. If you don't believe it, watch what happens in a bar. If a bunch of men really get into a good conversation, they'll talk all night. There may be girls all around the place, and yet they won't split off and go over by the girls if they've got a good conversation going. They'll just stay there and talk.

Getting a Foot in the Door

People ask, "But how in the world do you get in? What do you do? How do you establish contacts?" I think you have to begin by realizing that most of these nightclubs and bars are public places. Although they are privately owned, they are open to the public. So it's not much of a problem to get in. However, staying in or being able to come back may be a different story. And it is basically your behavior that sets the pace. It's your attitude. If you are too aggressive and self-righteous, you won't get in to many. They will kick you out. But if you just love people and share Jesus Christ, they'll let you run wild. You've got to cool it a little bit.

If I wake up in the middle of the night and I'm kind of restless I say, "Thank you, Jesus." The Lord must want me to run out and talk to somebody. I don't just lay there in bed rolling around and feeling sorry for myself because I can't sleep. I either get up and study the Bible or I go out and drive around. There will be someone out there on the street that needs to be talked to. He is lonely, wishing for someone to come along and spend a little time with him.

I find that if I am considerate to a lonely night person here and there, I have no trouble developing a permanent ministry. The last time we came back to Hollywood, inside of three weeks we were working in about forty places. About forty bars, pornographic bookstores, night clubs that would let us come back. We got to know the bartender, the manager, the waitresses, and they said, "Welcome back, come in any time you want." Isn't that amazing? It's wonderful. They all know that we don't agree with the behavior and everything else that goes on in these places, and yet they welcome us back. And, we're sharing Jesus Christ. It would take all the time of several people to just keep visiting and witnessing and sharing Christ with the patrons and owners of those forty places.

Get the Feel of the Place

There are a lot of things you can do to get a feel of the neighborhood. When I go to Sunset Strip, I like to turn my car radio to a rock 'n roll station quite loud. I go rocking down Sunset Strip to get my mind and my ears tuned in to what I am going to experience. The Sunset Strip people are groovers. They are into themselves. Every girl down there thinks she is the grooviest thing in Hollywood. Now, they don't know that the people who are down on Hollywood Boulevard and Western don't feel that way. They have a more realistic evaluation of themselves, bordering on despising themselves. The crowd that is now on Sunset will be on Hollywood and Western a year or two later. But for the time being they are kind of grooving down there. So when I go into a rock 'n roll place, I step inside and get my ears in tune with the music. I slowly take in the whole scene. I don't just go diving in. I ease in and stand there for a while until I kind of get the beat of the place. If there are a whole bunch of dudes standing around with dark glasses kind of really grooving, I may say, "Hey, man, let me turn you on." I develop an attitude that I'm a dealer for Jesus.

But if I'm in a piano bar late at night down on Melrose or in the Hollywood area and there is a little quiet piano playing and a lot of people gathered around, I wouldn't go in and say, "Wow, man, how's it going?" That wouldn't fit in. I would be totally out of the scene. People go to the kinds of places that fit their personalities. Personally, at this kind of piano bar, I want to be quiet. I don't want bam, bam, bam music. I don't want to be around a bunch of teenie boppers. The piano bar fits a certain mood. In a place like that I just quietly go over to someone sitting on a back stool. I sort of half sit down and say, "I'd like to give you one of these handbills. How's it going tonight? Oh, not too good? I'm a Christian and I would just like to give you one of these 'Turn on to Jesus' stickers." The manager may ask, "What are you doing giving this stuff out here?" "Well, I'm just a Christian sharing about the Lord. One night I prayed and invited Jesus to come into my heart." My voice is quiet, and I'm talking to one person in a way that he can understand.

At another club where the music is vibrating my ears out, I come on strong. I can't say much, because they can't understand. They can only see my lips going. They see the sticker and they'll take it. They'll take just about anything in those places. People are body to body. I may cup my hand and say (real loud), "Are you saved?" "What?" There's no point in saying, "How are you, and how's it going?" The environment's hot and heavy and everybody's joking around. He may finally hear me. "Am I saved?" "Yes, Jesus loves you." You have to scream above the music about Jesus. That's about all you can do in there.

Some Clubs Are a Special Challenge

If you go into a club where there are dancers on stage, you can't go in and just start working from person to person. The waitresses and the managers have their eyes open for people who come in and don't want to buy a drink but just want to watch the girls. They usually have a one- or two-drink minimum to avoid this. So, if you go in and don't buy a drink, they'll catch you quickly and throw you out. I always go to the bar right away in a place like that. I talk to the waitress or ask for the manager, and then I tell them what I'm doing there. If they don't mind my standing around, then I can start talking with people. But you just can't go in and start working from person to person because they'll think you're one of the freaks who are just trying to watch the girls and not buy drinks.

And then there are clubs where they have a door fee, and you've got to pay to get in. The fee is usually super high and you can't get in until you pay. So you have to use another angle to get in. Sometimes if you get into one, you can get into the others because that owner tells you whom to see. If you're trying to develop a permanent ministry, the best thing to do is to see the owner or the manager right away. The person who is going to be most responsive as a general rule is the one who owns the place, because he can't get fired for letting you in. Workers who are afraid of their jobs are more protective than the manager or the owner.

Make a Key Contact

It's best to start with a club that has the owner's name in its title. If you were new to the area and you saw Gazzarri's Hollywood-A-Go-Go, you might say to yourself, "Gazzarri, that sounds like someone's name." You might ask someone outside, "Is Gazzarri the man that owns this place?" And they would say, "Yes, Bill Gazzarri." Then you could walk in and say to the guy standing at the door (who's paid not to let you in), "I'd like to see Bill Gazzarri". . . just like he's an old friend of yours. There's a good chance the guy will let you in. You get to meet the owner. Now, that doorman wouldn't let you go to witness. He would think you were just trying to con him out of the door fee. But if the owner lets you in, it's O.K.

Of course, Bill Gazzarri threw me out a number of times back in 1967 and early 1968. I would come to the door and he'd say, "Get him out, get him out, go on out of here, man. This is my church. Get out of here, preacher." But I kept going back once a week or so. One night there weren't many people inside, and I said, "Bill, I've got something to ask you about." He said, "I thought I told you to stay out of here, preacher." I said, "Listen, what's your lowest night, when the fewest people are in here?" And he said, "Hmmm, Tuesday nights." I said, "What time Tuesday nights?" "Oh, about 10 til 12. Something like that." I said, "Let me preach in here on Tuesday night and I guarantee we will pack it out." I could see his mind start calculating. "My door fee . . ." he said, "I'll still charge." I said, "Do whatever you want to do, but how about it?" "I have to think about it." He thought it over a while, and then finally agreed. We were in, and we finally wound up doing gospel rallies there. I called on Andrae Crouch, who was then with Teen Challenge, for some music. Nobody knew Andrae Crouch then, but he had some good soul singing. Then, we got Charles McPheters and other groups. We had two-hour rallies in there on Tuesday nights. I still go into Gazzarri's all the time and that was years ago.

Then when you know one owner, you can ask who owns this place or that place. He may be willing to vouch for you and tell the others that you've been cooperative and haven't hurt his business. In time the network will spread to all the clubs.

Be a Friend to Celebrities

It always helps to know someone. It holds true with all kinds of celebrities, with nightclub singers, with members of motorcycle gangs, etc. These people want to know that you are solid. They want to know that they can be proud of you. Now that may sound strange, but many celebrities want to know they have a preacher friend or a Christian friend, and they want one that they can be proud of. I've been a guest at the Artist and Model's Ball and have come to some of the biggest parties in Hollywood. People have wanted me to go and be seen with them. Sometimes they do it just for their own publicity, but that's O.K. They want to feel that they can be proud to have you as their friend. That doesn't mean that you can't witness while you're with them. You can put stickers everywhere. They will groove on it.

I used to go every year to the Artist and Model's Ball. I'd wear a "Rapture Suit," a red suit. I called it that because they'd have black lights and the suit would glow with "Smile God Loves You" all over it. I wore a helmet with "Jesus Loves You" on it, carried a Bible that had a psychedelic cover, and I'd give out red stickers. On the back of the suit was a sign that said "Rapture Suit." I still have it. Of course, that was in keeping with the occasion. Everyone was in costume, body paint, and all that kind of stuff. It's a really weirdo, freak-out atmosphere. If I had worn a suit and tie, they wouldn't have let me in. So I came blazing in in my "Rapture Suit," glowing in the black light, and everyone said, "Wow, what a suit that is. Wow, what trip are you into?" I said, "I'm for real; Jesus loves you." Then they would say, "What's a Rapture Suit?" I'd respond, "When the Lord comes, are you going to be ready?" I had the opportunity to witness all night. But it took grooving just a little bit. They didn't mind asking me back to their next thing or to someone's party. They'd say, "Bring the preacher along. He's more fun than anyone else." I didn't mind if they felt, "This is a ding-bat preacher that doesn't know anything."

Not Everyone Feels Comfortable in a Bar

Some people are so out of touch with the nightlife culture that they can never minister effectively in bars. They feel self-righteous and judgmental toward the people they're trying to reach.

I have a great advantage over most people. When I was

four years old, my dad came home from World War II, and I started living in bars and clubs. As a little kid I was sitting on bar stools hour after hour after hour, listening to jukebox music. When I walk into a bar, I feel at home. I really do, mentally, emotionally, psychologically. I feel more at home there than I do in most of the churches I preach in. The environment brings back childhood memories. I feel like I know those people, though I've never met them before. I feel like I know how to talk to them. I feel like I've been made out of the same stuff they are. I feel like we're together. I really do. By contrast, when I'm in strange cities and go into a church and don't know anybody, the environment is so stiff that I feel uncomfortable. It's easier walking into the old dive around the corner, because I know what to do in there. I say this to explain the advantage I have over some people who try such a ministry. I think God uses me in this area because I do have a comfortable feeling about it. The people in these places are not strangers. It wasn't that one day when I was 35 years old I started trembling and said, "I've got to go into a bar and witness to those strangers in there." I've lived with them throughout my life. I've gone into thousands of clubs.

Sometimes when I've been carrying the cross along a hot, dusty road, I see a bar, an old country dive. Boy I'm thirsty and need something to drink. I wheel up and lean the cross up against the side of the door. The people in the bar watch me. I come in and get a coke and start passing out stickers and tracts. "What in the world is that outside?" "Oh, that's my cross. I'm going along the road sharing Jesus. Ya'll want to see it?" I go out and bring it right in the door, and we have a good time talking about Jesus.

Have Respect for Every Person

If you don't respect the people you're witnessing to, they'll know it. If you look down your nose at them, you'll never get anywhere.

I remember when we were demonstrating against the Classic Cat. We had a little girl down on Sunset Strip carrying a sign—"Do you want your daughter topless too?" After we did our marching, I put the signs away and the owner said, "Come on in, Arthur; you really socked it to us tonight." I said, "Yeah, we're going to get this place closed down. Praise the Lord." Then the manager said, "Blessitt, you're really after us. I hope you never move down in front of those other topless clubs. Get all the publicity for the Classic Cat that you can get. Tell them that we're the best sinners in town." We'd just been out there fighting them, and yet we were friends because they knew I loved them. Our purposes were totally different, but they felt I was their friend.

This kind of relationship is possible when your attitude is not that of condemnation, but of concern. Jesus let a sinner woman, who was a stranger to Him, come along and wash His feet. We've no idea who the woman was, but when Jesus was eating in the respectable man's house, the Bible says, "There came a woman who was a sinner, and while he was eating she began to wash His feet with her tears, and bathed them with the hairs of her head, and kissed His feet." They started condemning Him, so Jesus said, "I came into your house and you didn't anoint my feet, but she did. You didn't give me any kisses, but she has not stopped kissing my feet." It wasn't just one kiss. She was sitting there, holding onto His feet, kissing them, drying them with her hair and weeping. This went on all the while Jesus was still eating and He spent a period of time there. It wasn't an instant thing. We know she had been there for a while because they were questioning Him about why He let her continue to do it to Him. Then He said to her, "Thy sins are forgiven thee. Go thy way. Thy faith hath saved thee." What I'm pointing out is that Jesus was a friend of publicans and sinners. He was able to let that woman relate freely to Him because she knew His holiness and she accepted it.

Most of the people who are involved in — I hate to use the word — gross sin (there may be many sins in the church grosser than these; they're just not as open) do not need to be told how bad they are. What they need to be told is how good Jesus is, and how wonderful His love is and what He can do. Most of them will then begin to tell you how bad they are. They know how bad they are. I have been with my dad night after night when he was drinking. He would sit there on the bar stool and tell me how bad he had been to my mother, how mean he had been to the kids, how awful he was to everybody around him. Yet, when he was sobered up the next day, you'd think he lived a better life than the preacher. Many people are more honest when they're drunk than when they're sober. When they're drunk, they tell you how bad they are. And when they're sober they tell you how good they are, because they don't want to face the truth. When people see the holiness of Christ, that reveals the wickedness of their own soul. If you're pastoring a church, and you want to get the people under conviction of sin, give them a glimpse of Jesus and they'll be crying under conviction. They'll recognize more sin through seeing Jesus than they will if you preach a sermon on evil. I'm not saying that you shouldn't talk about evil when you're dealing with a person who doesn't understand his lost condition. But as a general policy, go with the good news, go sharing hope.

When Opportunity Knocks . . .

It's important to take advantage of every opportunity. If a club has a band on stage, you can ask the manager if you can speak for a few minutes between band set changes. Sometimes they'll let you. If the owner or manager is Catholic, it's usually much easier to get in than if he is Protestant or Jewish. Catholics have much more respect for the ministry. You might phrase it differently. "May I bring an evening devotion?" They're not sure what a devotion is but it sounds spiritual. "I'd like just to bring a five minute devotion, just before you close, or between one of the dance sets." They may just let you go up there. Take advantage of anything that's happening. If you get a brainstorm that something ought to be done, try it. Nothing's lost.

If you start taking advantage of every kind of thing that's happening in your town, you'll be amazed what opens up. If someone says, "We're having a big party over here . . . got 50 or 75 of us . . . and smoking grass . . . big grass party . . . will you come along?" You say, "I don't smoke, I just burn for the Lord. If there's any room for a soul saver, I'd be glad to come along." "Ha, ha, well come along, we've never had a preacher at our party." Go in, take advantage of it . . . it's an opportunity. You can dive in and start witnessing. If they don't want you, they'll ask you to leave. But they brought you; they invited you. You can usually stay in the main room. It's in the other rooms that bad things may be happening.

But watch what you're drinking and remember what you're there for. If you are known as a Christian witness, then there may be people trying to turn you on. Or there may be a punch drink that's high. Drink a bottle of coke to be sure. A person may offer you a drink from *his* bottle of coke, but someone may have dropped a little touch of acid in there, so buy and open your own. You have to be careful about this, because you only have to get wasted away once, and it can put a scandal over you for the rest of your ministry. So don't take any chances.

You have to be careful of drugs in other ways too. If someone asks you to take a package down and mail it for him, just don't get involved in it. It's liable to be full of cocaine, or heroin, or something else, and it may be a set-up and you'd be arrested. You've got to be wise and think about what you're getting into. Watch yourself. Be sensitive. Pray for the discernment to know what's going on. That's what's involved in being street wise. If this is your ministry, you've got to be able to know what's happening, what's moving, what the scene is, what's going on. You've got to be at home with the street.

Make Them Remember You

I also suggest that if you're starting a permanent ministry, you find some way for people to identify you easily. In the years past on the Strip, we always had cards printed. We didn't pass them out just to impress everybody. It gave them a way to remember us, and it showed them that we were in the community to stay. They came to trust the people who carry your ministry's card. Someone else may come along who is not connected with you, and they won't let them in. "No, I've got somebody else who comes in here and ministers." You've gained a confidence and a reputation and an image, and that's important, whether you're in a small town or a big city. It will determine what the people of that place think of you. They may not want to be buddy-buddy, but they'll know you're O.K.

Cultivate a Good Reputation

We may misunderstand the Bible verse that says Jesus "made Himself of no reputation." He spent three years of ministry building a reputation, as a friend of publicans and sinners, as a mighty worker for God. Because of His reputation, many came to believe that He was the Messiah. Even those who had never met Him wanted to meet Him. They knew that He was preaching the gospel of the Kingdom, and healing every sickness and disease among the people. They knew that all over Israel. So you too need to develop a reputation.

Here's something that will help you build an honest reputation: Don't make an obligation to anyone unless you can keep it. They'll respect you more if you make no promises or commitments than they will if you say you can do something and don't do it. If someone comes up to you and says, "Can you get me a place to spend the night?" and you look at them and say, "No, I don't know of any place available," that person may be your friend for weeks and months and years. But if you tell him, "Let me see if I can; I think maybe I can," he thinks you've made a promise; you've given an indication that you can help him. When you don't produce, he'll say, "Boy, that guy lied to me. I waited five hours for that dud; thought he was going to get me a place to spend the night and he didn't." Before you know it, the word has been spread all over the community. If you do that a few times, everyone on the street will say you're a liar. That's all it takes, just a few times.

If you're in a club, it's best to say, "I'll drop back in the next two weeks," or, "I'll be back . . . I make the rounds once in a while." If you say, "I'll be back Thursday night," you'd better be back Thursday night. If you can't, call and let them know. Don't begin breaking your word in the street. Be vague if you need to, and people will accept it. But if you say something, then DO IT. That's how you develop a reputation of honesty and earn their trust and respect.

I often have people ask me, "Can you lead me in Bible study?" With my schedule I know I can't do it, so I say, "No, I don't have the time, but I know who can." I'll get in touch with some person I trust, and they can teach them the Bible. But if I tell them I'm going to lead them in Bible study, but I just never get around to it, they'll lose confidence in me, and it will hurt them. Just try to decide what you *can* do, and don't do any more than that. Don't make obligations to do more than you can carry out, because you'll be more effective at the things you do commit yourself to do.

A One-Night Blitz

There is also a place for witnessing in bars and clubs where you're not planning to maintain a permanent ministry. This may be approached differently. If you're going to Jackson, Mississippi, or Chicago and you're only going to be there for two nights, you don't have time to waste trying to figure out who runs this place or that place or the other place. Just go into one and start at the back. That way, if they throw you out, you can deal tracts out the door. Besides, it's usually less noisy back there and you're less obvious to the management. You can just give out materials or you can go up to the tables and share.

Sometimes I've ministered in Las Vegas when I was just there for a short while. I might go back to a blackjack table in a gambling casino. The dealer's dealing out cards and I say, "I'd like to give you one of these." I give them each a tract, then I say, "Thank you so much," turn and walk away fast. It stops the whole game. They may have been concentrating on blackjack, but now they open the tract and start to read. "Where did he go? There's a nut in here." And I go zigzagging between the rows of slot machines. I come across one of those little change slots where the money's coming out and stick a tract in there. I don't do it in every row. I may skip four rows, because they'll be trailing me by now. I fake them out. I hit there. I hit here. If they catch me and throw me out, Praise the Lord. I may be gone, but my literature is in there anyway. And then I'll hit the next joint.

You can blitz a town in this way in one or two nights. You just go to all the clubs and the bars. Start at the back and go up to every table. "I'd like to give you all one of these. Jesus loves you. Do you know Christ in your heart?" Many times you can almost take over. A lot of the places will let you keep doing it indefinitely. But in others, you're liable to be run out. It doesn't matter, if you're just there for one night. Move from place to place. Blitz that town with the gospel. You may be thrown out of a certain place, but you can send your buddy in. "They haven't told *you* to leave yet. You hit this one, and I'll move on down the street." Or you may feel led to go back in yourself. Sometimes a place will run you out two or three times, but the fourth time they let you stay. It may be wide open for you to witness and share.

The Gospel in a Porn Shop

Pornography shops provide a special opportunity. A lot of the guys working the late night shift in these places are really lonely, and they're hungry to have somebody decent to talk to. It's a wonderful place to witness, especially if there's a girl with your ministering group. They're so sick of seeing all the sex perverts pouring in that they're just glad to see someone who's an honest, good, nice person. They love to talk. They'll talk to a guy or a girl. You have to be considerate of their business if you're planning to have a continuing ministry there. If you're not planning to go back, do anything you want. Be considerate if you're trying to build a relationship for the future. If you're talking to the manager and a customer comes up with an old porno magazine in his hand wanting to buy it, step out of the way so that he can go ahead with his business. You don't agree with the fact that he's selling this stuff but if you stand there and you're blocking the customers, before long he's going to have to get mad and send you out, and then you won't be able to come back. So you can stand out of the way when he's waiting on a customer and then give him a little brochure to put in the package too.

Go as far as you can the first time, and then back out with the door open. If the guy says, "I just don't know if we can stand much of the witnessing in here or not," reply, "Well, listen, I appreciate your letting me come and share, and in another few nights I'll be back in to talk to you again. The guy was just fixing to throw you out, but you've thanked him for letting you in, and you've invited yourself back without giving him a chance to say no. The door's still open. When you make your visit the next time, say, "How ya doin', Al?" (Get their names if you can. Write them down so you remember.) If you come in as if you are an old friend, they usually accept you that way.

The Gospel in a Massage Parlor

Massage parlors are one of those fads that come and go. The government may come up with some kind of ordinance that will wipe them out for a while, but then they will find a way around the ordinance and flourish again. A lot of scenes go through this cycle. Right now massage parlors are down. Praise the Lord. There are still some around, but you generally have to have a contact inside to do any witnessing there. Some of the massage parlors have a straight person sitting at the desk. A client makes the deal and he never sees the girl until he goes in. In others, you walk into a lounge and the girls will all be sitting around, wanting to talk to you. Then the client makes the deal after he's met them. So your approach depends on the massage parlor set-up.

If there is just one guy at the desk, then you won't be able to get in to see the girls unless you get past him. You can do that by sharing and talking with him, getting to be his friend, coming back again and again. If you do this regularly, there is very little problem. You become a familiar part of the street scene to them. They'll understand who you are and what you're doing. Soon you'll just be able to say, "I'd like to go in and talk to some of the girls and give them a sticker." "Well, I don't know if they'd be interested." "Let me try it anyway." And they'll let you go ahead and do it. It usually works out very well if you're in an area on a permanent basis. When you're making a one-night blitz in a strange town, you just have to press as far as you can and then back off. You've got to remember that this is a private business in a private building, so you have to leave when they ask you to.

Go Two by Two

As a rule, I think it's best to go two by two when you're witnessing in night spots. A partner gives most people added encouragement and security. If more than two people hit one bar at once, it looks like God's taking over. It scares the people and they won't be open for conversations.

Sometimes when we're out on the street at night and there are six or eight of us, I'll say, "A couple of you go in here, and then another couple hit this bar, and this one. . . ."

Now, as a matter of personal preference, I enjoy working alone, because then I don't have to worry about anyone else. I just keep my mind on what I'm doing. But I don't recommend that for everyone. Two by two usually works best.

Even though you go out two by two, witnessing is always best when it's done by one person. When I'm working in a bar, it bothers me to be talking to someone while a third party, the Christian who is in the bar with me, stands nearby so he can hear what's being said. It upsets the person I'm witnessing to, and it upsets me. In a bar, it just doesn't seem right to have a third party standing around. On the streets it's O.K. We train people on the street by letting them listen in while someone experienced witnesses. But it just doesn't work in a bar. People become sensitive as to what that person is doing. "Why is he listening? What is he up to?"

Should You Smoke, Drink, Dance?

Those of us who work in street ministry come face to face with the fact that in the world we are dealing with a variety of cultures. Christians have a wide range of various convictions, personal convictions of what's right and wrong, whether Christians should smoke or drink any alcoholic beverage or dance, etc. I don't want to get into the details; that would take a separate book. But, I'll tell you my own personal principle of operation. Don't let your practices stand in the way of your ministry. If you smoke, I would advise you not to do it when you're out witnessing and working in the clubs and bars. If you drink moderately and feel that's all right, don't drink in the clubs you're ministering in and working with. If you're working with a club and you're sharing with people and you feel like getting up and dancing, I would advise you not to do it. It will be very difficult to witness and to maintain an outreach ministry if you suddenly do something that makes them feel that you're just like them. I'm not saying what's right and wrong. I'm speaking practically. I've just found over and over again that it's most effective not to participate in anything that's part of the scene you're witnessing in.

Here's What Can Happen

Does witnessing in bars and nightclubs pay off? Here's the answer straight from the horse's mouth. Ron Bozarth was the manager of a popular night spot on Sunset Strip. This is his personal testimony:

"We had the only 'class' topless place in the business. Isn't that something to brag about? But we were very proud of it truthfully. In reality, this 'class' place was really a cesspool, the dregs of everything that could happen on the street. I'm not trying to take this as a badge of honor; I'm trying to explain to you that even the best of such places is awful. There wasn't anything you couldn't get in our place. If you wanted to get somebody killed, you could do it there. Literally killed. If there was anything you wanted to buy, you could get it in our place. And we had *the* 'class' place. And I, with my ego, was the 'class' operator, the manager of the place.

"At that time, about 1968, the Strip was covered with hippies. Now, we didn't like the hippies, obviously, because they didn't have any money. But they had a habit of falling asleep in our driveway or in front of the place. It was really a problem. We couldn't just throw them out. We tried. We hired people to get rid of them, but they kept coming back. They didn't have any place to go. One night, I'll never forget it, we had a line of people, paying customers, waiting to get in. The place was packed. The doorman came up to me and said, 'Ron, there's a guy who wants to talk to the manager.' I figured it was another complaint or maybe someone willing to spend a little money to get in and get a seat. And, I said, 'Okay. Fine,' and walked over. Along came this bouncing, smiling, long-haired, hippie freak.

"He came up with his Bible in his hand, and he said, 'Hi, I'm Arthur Blessitt.' He stuck out his hand and grabbed my hand to shake it. I thought, 'Oh boy. We've got a yo-yo here.' And he said, 'I just wanted to ask you a question.' I was trying to get rid of him, to get loose from him, but he kept holding on. And there were people all around. I was the boss, and this long-haired, Bible-toting guy with stickers all over him, was holding onto me.

"Arthur said, 'Ron, I want to know if you know Jesus Christ.' A lot of you may think that if you approach someone like that, they're going to think you're foolish. They may at first. I was embarrassed and I'm sure I said something kind of smart. But there was a difference. As I look back 10 years ago, I realize that the difference was that Arthur Blessitt walked in with a glow on. He was just beaming. No one in the club who was supposed to be turned on was shining like that.

"He kept holding onto me, and he said, 'Ron, boy, you're the manager of this place. I said, 'Yeah.' He said, 'Wow, what a job this must be, running all these people.' He knew just how to get to me. 'Yeah, well, I run the whole place.' I was real proud of it. And he said, 'Ron, all these girls—(We had five stages going around, with nude women on all the stages. Also, there were bars operating and the waitresses had very little on.) Where do they go when they come off the stage?' I said, 'Oh, we have a dressing room in the back.' He was still holding onto me, and I was really feeling embarrassed to be standing next to him. I was in a tuxedo, he was in beads.

"Then Arthur said, 'Ron, I wonder if it would be all right

if I talked to a couple of the girls when they come off stage.' And I thought, 'Boy, wouldn't that be something?' I said, 'Arthur, you don't want to talk to them.' These were pretty rough girls. They'd been around for a long time. But he said, 'I'd like to go wherever they go and talk to them' Well, at any given time our dressing room in the back had girls there, all nude, all into everything you can imagine.

"I couldn't shake Arthur, so I took him back there, thinking, 'This is going to be like throwing Daniel into the lions' den. I knew that I was putting him into something that he couldn't cope with. I opened the door, and I said, 'Girls, there's a guy here who wants to talk to you.' I pushed him in and closed the door, and I went back to work. I was laughing to myself. I went up to the bartender and said, 'You ain't going to believe this; I've got a preacher back there in the girls' dressing room.'

"Well, the girls were dancing and coming off the stages by rotation, and all of a sudden I noticed there was an empty stage over here. And there was another empty stage. Before long, I had a lot of empty stages and a lot of irate customers. I went back to the dressing room to see what was going on and here were all of my leading nude dancers, that I'd brought in from Vegas and San Francisco and other places, and they were all sitting there with something covering them. And Arthur was talking to them.

"I think it's important that I make the point that he was talking to them. He wasn't having a prayer meeting, he was just talking to them. He was doing something that was really unique. He was being a friend to them, and friendship is not something you come by very often in that business. You may have a lot of acquaintances, but not many friends. Arthur was being a friend. Well, I had a real problem. I couldn't get any of the girls to go on stage. They were really interested. Then he started talking about Jesus Christ, and some of them suddenly began to go. Yet, they weren't dancing like they used to. They were very tame, and the show went to pot.

"I realized that I had to get Arthur out of there, so I said, 'Come on, I want you to meet my bartenders.' I had two winners, two real tough bartenders there. Those guys could handle anything. I took Arthur over and introduced them to him. And then I split again. I got the girls back on stage, though the show was not very good at all that night. But I saw Arthur over there, standing by the bar with his Bible laying on the bar, drinking a coke. Before long I noticed that one bartender wasn't pouring drinks. Instead he was talking to Arthur. This just went on and on.

"Finally, I realized that there was only one thing to do to keep the club going and that was for *me* to talk to Arthur. So I went back to Arthur and said, 'Come on, let's go over here and talk.' Well, this thing kept bothering me, this glow about the man. I know now that this glow is called Jesus Christ, and it was like an aura around him.

"You know, Arthur made a friend of everyone in that club, and there's a reason why. The reason Arthur Blessitt got through to so many of us in the nightclub business is because Arthur never once judged us. Never! He recognized, I think, with the help of the Lord, the fact that all of us who are in this business (I'm out of that work now) have the same basic problem—loneliness.

"I didn't start off in the nightclub business. I came from a very religious home with two beautiful parents. I used to make jokes on the stage about the fact that I could probably never be successful because I came from the right side of the tracks. However, my church didn't give me much help. It was a church that preached that everyone was going to hell except them. Christ said He was going to prepare a place for us, and my feeling as a young man was that He shouldn't have been gone so long. We didn't need much room. Only our church was going to be there, and I couldn't imagine why it was taking Him so long. Later I saw this judgmental spirit for what it was, so I got away from it.

"Throughout the years I was in the nightclub business, I

saw the church only as a group of people saying, 'You're a sinner. You're bad.' Now, along came Arthur and his type of ministry, and they weren't judging, they were offering friendship, and offering a better way. That's what Christians have to offer unbelievers — friendship and a better way."

Ron Bozarth is now a beautiful Christian. At his wedding, when I married him and his wife, Jerry, we knelt together and they both gave their lives to Jesus before they took their marriage vows. Ron is no longer in the nightclub business. Praise God! He is a strong testimony for Jesus. The arm of God is not short and He can save anyone from any condition.

2

WITNESSING WHEREVER YOU ARE

4
Jesus in Your Neighborhood

The Logical Place to Begin

How are we going to be an effective witness in the world if we don't begin in our own neighborhood? Everyone of us lives somewhere, and wherever we live, that's where our witness for Jesus should begin. It shouldn't just happen when we go out on the streets to tell people about Jesus, or when we go off to another city for a crusade. Nor should it begin when the church gives us a prospect card to follow-up. Our first responsibility is to evangelize the neighborhood where we eat and sleep, where our children go to school.

Each of us needs to think about where the potential is in his neighborhood, to analyze the opportunities of witness that are available to him. I've done that kind of an analysis of the street scene in Hollywood, and our ministry there is the result. I've analyzed the community, the potential for witness where the people are, when they are present in the largest numbers. I try to regulate my schedule so that I'll be the most efficient witness for Jesus Christ possible. You can do this in your neighborhood as well. I'm not talking about the whole city, just the limited neighborhood surrounding you, where you do your shopping, where you get your hair done, where you go to school.

List on a sheet of paper all the restaurants, the bars, the shopping centers, the beauty parlor, the laundromat, the convenience store, the apartment house complex, the residential blocks, etc. Put these all down and then look at your list and see where your present witness is now. Are you being effective in reaching that neighborhood now? Then work out a plan for witnessing there more consistently. This will give you a strategy to follow.

Your Church as the Base of Operation

I would encourage you to think of the reaching of your neighborhood for Christ as the normal function of your church as a united group of Christians. There are some places that cannot be reached by a single local church, such as downtown L.A. or New York, or the beaches and other resorts. But normally it ought to be thought of as the job of your church to reach the fields that are ripe with the harvest near you.

Every local church should be sensitive and adaptable, because each neighborhood is unique. The pastor ought to be the leader in developing the church's evangelistic vision. But he cannot do all the work himself. It is impossible for him to pastor the church and also to be personally involved in every area where evangelism is needed. He won't be able to study the Bible and have something fresh to preach and teach every week, or to counsel with those who need counsel, or to bury those who are dying, or to marry those who are being married, or to lead the services, etc. One person simply can't do it. Even in the early church this was recognized. They said, "We've got to set ourselves apart for prayer and fasting and ministering the Word of God, and some others will have to be appointed to look after other needs."

Everyone Part of the Evangelistic Team

An effective program of evangelism can develop in your church. The pastor should be at the hub. Then there will be someone who is in charge of street ministry, because he has felt a particular burden to work in the bars and in the streets. Another person may be in charge of tract distribution. Another may be in charge of gathering all the Christian magazines that people aren't using any more and putting them in doctors' offices, at laundromats, at the bus station, at the airport, etc., changing the supplies weekly. Another person may be the leader with door-to-door evangelism constantly reaching the homes around the church. Someone else may coordinate the visiting of people who have attended church and are good prospects. Someone else may be involved in a ministry to the jail and the juvenile hall. Another person may be involved in convalescent home and hospital evangelism.

The pastor should meet together with these leaders every two weeks or so for prayer and sharing. The pastor himself can rotate from one ministry to another, go out a bit with this group, then this group, then this group. This will keep him aware of what's happening. Then, all the other people in the church should become involved in one or another of these outreaches. Such a team approach can be an instrument of reaching out into the entire area around a church with effective witness.

Any church which has a ministry of outreach evangelism will also have to develop a plan for outreach follow-up. If you're leading people to the Lord in shopping centers and homes and stores and bars, you're going to have to have some people in the church whose main ministry is follow-up. They will get new believers started in a Bible study and in church attendance. This is how the whole body works together, evangelizing, following up, teaching and instructing. If our churches functioned effectively in this way, there would be little need for people like me. The local people would already have the area saturated. That's the ideal kind of evangelism — the whole body and fellowship of Christ trying to reach their entire neighborhood for Jesus Christ.

Your Home Can Be an Outreach Center

It's amazing how much witnessing can be done right in

your own home. All sorts of people knock at your door, and you should be prepared to share Jesus with them.

Why not put a tract rack next to your front door? Or just a little display of tracts on a table nearby? Then when a salesman knocks on your door, you open it. They have a little something to sell, and you say, "Well, I don't really think I can use that today, but I'll tell you what I can do. I've got a little something I want you to read, a little brochure to give you." Give them the material and then unload the gospel on them. By doing this you'll get to witness to every religious group that works neighborhoods. You'll get to witness to every pot and pan salesman, every yard mower who wants a job. You've just got the potential for evangelism at your door and all you have to do is have your material nearby and ready for you to work with.

Anyone who works on or around your house — the gardeners, the street crews, the plumber — is an opportunity for witness placed before you by God. You should feel thankful to Jesus that He allowed this gas heater to break down, or that He allowed you to have the money to build this addition. Now you have all these carpenters and repairmen and you can share with them about Jesus Christ. A nice approach with people who have been working on your house is to invite them to have a cup of coffee. They'll almost always accept a cup of coffee or hot tea or something cold on a warm afternoon. Then give them a tract or a New Testament and say, "I really appreciate what you've done and I'd like to share with you a word about my own experience with Jesus Christ." This is a very effective way of witnessing.

A Missionary to the Pagan Tribes at Your School

Think of how many unbelievers you rub shoulders with when you go to school. Opportunities to witness are all around you. You'll usually find clusters of kids sitting around the campus during lunch hour, telling dirty jokes, smoking, talking about yesterday's ballgame. You can just pass the word around through these groups that you're going to have a Jesus meeting over there under the tree. If some of your friends gather with you, you can have a spontaneous and unorganized sort of a rally, Bible study or prayer meeting right there during noon hour. Now, don't let it become an exclusive Christian club, where only the holy holies meet together and no one else feels comfortable. Make sure it has the kind of atmosphere that is attractive to other students. You'll be amazed at the sharing and Bible study that can grow out of such a spontaneous meeting.

On many campuses you can start before school prayer meetings. Many of these have to be very short, and their purpose is mainly to be an encouragement for the Christians. At other schools, you will be able to have club meetings during your free period. You may form a Bible club though you can probably find a better name for it. You usually need permission and a faculty sponsor. If a club is impossible during school hours, you may be able to start an after-school Bible study on the campus in an empty room. Or you may have an after-school Bible study or Bible club in an adjoining church or some other building right by the school. Don't try to do this very far away from the school or you'll lose them. It's got to be right at the school so that some of the kids can drop by on their way home. You'll always need to run these on time or the parents will begin to keep their kids from coming. If a kid says I'm going to be 30 minutes late, and is 45 minutes late, some mothers worry and they won't ever get to come back in. Another effective technique is for you to share Jesus over lunch with your friends in the school cafeteria. Don't waste any of the great opportunities available at school.

Is There a Shopping Center Near You?

There is a lot of similarity between witnessing at a shopping center and street witnessing. But as far as the law is concerned, they're in a different category. They have to be approached differently. On the public sidewalk no one can forbid you to give out tracts or share Jesus so long as there's room for somebody to walk by and you're not blocking doorways to stores. But a shopping center is private property and has the right to monitor the activities that go on there. The U.S. Supreme Court ruled this way in a five-to-four decision. I disagree with their decision and I expect it to be reversed someday, but in the meantime, that's what the law is.

However, you will not be arrested right away. If they don't want you there, they will warn you. As a matter of fact, there are many that will allow you to do it, and there are even shopping centers that allow church groups to put loud speakers in the parking lot, free, and then to go through the mall witnessing. It just depends on the management of that shopping center. You'll never know until you try it.

Now, how do you witness in a shopping center? I've found that it's very natural to hit the parking lots first. There are several ways you can put gospel tracts on the outside of an automobile. You can bend the tract and stick it in the handle of the door, or you can slide one under the windshield wiper. But don't ever paste stickers on a car. You really create a havoc if somebody's done a fine painting job on his van and you put a sticker right over his artistic masterpiece. And many times they won't come off easily. So use tracts instead of stickers.

You can do personal witnessing in the parking lot too. Everyone inside the mall will be out in the parking lot sooner or later. As people look for their cars, you can walk up and talk with them.

Or you can go in and talk to the people sitting around in the mall. Give them a tract or just open your Bible. Many times I find that approach to be more effective inside the mall area than heavy literature distribution. If there is one person inside the mall who doesn't like Christians, he'll complain about all the materials. But if you aren't using a lot of material, just giving it to the people you are actually talking to, you almost totally eliminate the chance of getting run out of the shopping center. It's best not to use Jesus stickers in a shopping center because someone who doesn't like the sticker you gave him will put it on a store window. So, even if you're careful, they'll get in wrong places. Then the custodian or building manager will see all these red stickers and he'll begin to follow your trail. When he tracks you down, he'll want the stickers stopped because they're ruining his building, and he'll throw you out. And you could still have been witnessing in there if you had just eased along with your Bible talking and sharing with people inside the shopping mall.

Witnessing at Your Local Convenience Store

Most neighborhoods have a convenience store, such as the 7-11 markets. These places are open long hours, and I think the Lord's got those little stores going for late night witnesses. There's always someone to share with who's buying a few last minute items. You can always use a pack of chewing gum or a coke or peanuts or a penny piece of bubble gum. Any of these will give you an excuse to go in. Or you can just walk in and witness, without any intention of buying anything. If this little store is part of your normal pattern of life and you are a regular customer you can be almost sure that they will permit you to witness because they don't want to run off business.

Of course, you have to do it in a nice manner. You may dash in to get some milk, say to the guy behind the counter, "How's it going today? Say, are you going to heaven?" Give him a big grin and say, "I gave my life to Jesus several years ago, and He came in and saved me and has taken away my sin. I want to leave you this little thing to read. Keep it, and sometime when it's kind of quiet in here you can read the message." Then say, "Oh, would you like a sticker to put on the cash register? Or you can stick it in your billfold or something. Can I ask you a question? If you died this moment, do you have the assurance in your heart that you'd go to heaven? Do you know Jesus Christ as your Savior?" Quite often late at night, they're hungry to talk. And if the person isn't interested, just be pleasant and then witness again every time you can.

There are all kinds of ways of getting into conversations with customers. A person may be picking up a few things. You can say, "Looks like you're buying all the expensive food in the place. How much did the price go up since the last time?" Then say, "I'd like to give you a little tract that tells you about Jesus Christ. His prices haven't gone up at all. He still offers salvation free." It's better not to give him the tract cold. Chat with him a bit; share with him as a friend. Otherwise, he'll brush you off.

If someone isn't interested and says, "I'm in a hurry," you say, "Well, O.K., just stick it in your pocket and read it when you get a chance. God bless you. You'll see me around the store again. I shop here a lot. Love to talk to you another time. God bless you."

If you're paying for what you've bought by check, you can say to the clerk, "While I'm writing this check, why don't you read this?" Hand him a tract and then write very slowly. If you see they haven't gotten through it yet, you can make a mistake on the check, tear it up and start over. After they've read it, ask them if they're going to heaven. They may say, "I'm busy, I'm working." You say, "Well, you just keep the handbill and I'll be back again. I'll be glad to share with you, talk to you, pray with you anytime." That'll get them under conviction and everytime they see you coming, God will start dealing with them. Your very presence will make them think, "I wonder when he's going to get me?" Keep it nice and friendly and you'll have good results. Don't be belligerent or haughty or self-righteous. Have an attitude of loving and caring for everyone you meet and you will be able to share Jesus Christ wherever you go.

Sinners Come Clean at the Laundromat

You have to do your laundry. Why not combine it with witnessing? A laundromat is a great place to witness. There are always people sitting there with idle time. Twenty-four hours a day, lonely people. Often they are energetic people who have to sit around for an hour or more and do nothing. They'd rather be doing something else, but they've got to sit there until they can take the washed clothes out and put them in a dryer. They're just killing time so it's a beautiful place to witness. If you ever get an itch to witness, you can just leave the house for a while, run down to the laundromat. You'll almost always find someone there who will talk to you.

If there are four laundromats in your general area, take turns doing your laundry at each of them. That way you will hit a fresh crowd.

A pleasant, positive attitude will be your greatest tool in witnessing there. Be pleasant, be happy. Let them know that you've got a relationship with the Lord that's so wonderful they should just be dying to ask you about it. If your attitude is bright and cheerful, you can give them a tract and say, "Hey, how is it going in here today?" They may say it's hot in the laundromat, or comment on the weather. And you can say, "I've got a little brochure I'd like you to read while you're getting your laundry done." They'll almost always take it.

And because people are looking for something to read while they're waiting for their laundry, you can leave literature for those you don't hit personally. You can stick stickers inside the magazines, or you can lay some tracts where the magazines are. Don't leave a pile of tracts because it looks too "gospelly." And the guy who cleans the place will pick up all that religious stuff. But if you lay one here and there among all the papers and magazines, they'll stay. And sometimes late at night just go by and put a tract in each of the dryers. Some lady will bring it home. "Turn on to Jesus," or "If you died do you have the assurance you'd go to heaven?" She doesn't know where it came from, but she got it anyway.

If you are in a bad neighborhood, sometimes the drunks who don't have any place to sleep come in and lay down on a table in a laundromat and sleep. If the manager comes in, he will wake them up and run them out. I once found one of these guys laying on a table, and I led him to the Lord while he was still stretched out on the table. He never got up till after he was saved. I just went up to him and said, "I've got some good news for you tonight." He asked, "What good news?" I shared with him about Jesus Christ and he was saved.

You'll notice that most laundromats have telephones. So while you're there, decorate the phone a little. You can lift the receiver off the hook and put a Jesus sticker on the handle. Then when a person lifts the receiver, he's looking at it: "Smile, God Loves You." Don't put it over the part you speak into or over where you listen, because that agitates people. But a little sticker there on the handle doesn't bother anyone. A person about to commit suicide or anyone who is in trouble usually goes to the phone to call for help. If your car breaks down, if you are lonely, you make a phone call. If you are looking for something, you make a phone call. And there's that little old sticker right there on the handle.

Your Car, a Mobile Outreach Center

Your day-to-day neighborhood ministry should involve your car. It's good to have tracts and stickers handy all the time when you're driving. I use my ashtray for them since I don't smoke. It's a ready made tract-size slot. Some people hang a little plastic bag from their dashboard, but I like the ash tray. If you keep these tracts handy, then when you buy gas, you can easily reach over and pull out a tract.

You can also talk to the attendant about Jesus. Say, "Fill

'er up." Then add, "Are you full? Have you let Jesus fill your life? If that S fell off the Shell sign over your head, or a match fell in that gas tank, where would you go? To hell or to heaven?" That gets their attention. And while he's pumping gas, you can put literature in the restroom. Lay tracts around — or unroll the toilet tissue, put stickers on the paper and rewind the roll.

Even trouble can open opportunities for witnessing. My tape recorder broke one time. I don't know the plug-in from the motor on a machine, so I prayed about it. I said, "Lord fix this thing," but it didn't work. So finally I decided I had to have something done. I prayed and looked up a repair shop and finally found a guy who said he could work on my tape recorder. I took him the machine, and I gave him a gospel tract. He put the tract on the side, but I kept talking about Jesus. That didn't phase him at all. After he had been working on it for a while, he asked if I had a tape to test it.

I said, "Yes, yes, hallelujah." I wondered why I didn't think of that to begin with. So I gave him a tape of me preaching. When I gave it to him I was grinning from ear to ear. I said, "I think you'll get a blessing out of it too."

A few days later he called and said the tape recorder was fixed and I could come down and pick it up. When he gave it to me, he said, "I tell you, that preaching is as good as Billy Graham, but I don't think it's Billy Graham. Who is that preaching?" I said, "Well, did you like the sermon?" He said, "Yes, yes, that's good preaching. I like good preaching." I said, "Let me ask you this. Have you done what the sermon said?" He said, "Well, I'm not too religious myself." I said, "That fellow preaching is me." "You?" I started talking to him. I told him about Jesus and he gave his life to Jesus as we were both leaning across the counter.

After he was saved, I took a piece of chalk that was laying nearby and drew a big circle behind the counter. I put a little scrape mark on the wood in the middle of the circle. He asked, "What's that for?" I said, "Right here is where you accepted Christ, you will never forget it. That's holy ground, and everytime you step up to that counter, you'll remember you were saved and that you're a Christian.

One day the car motor burned out. I missed a meeting because of it. I said, "Praise the Lord. Jesus, you must have had us break down for a purpose." And, He did. I led the garage mechanic to Jesus Christ. He stayed up all night working on the motor, and the next morning when I went back to get the car he brought his wife down. They were preparing to get a divorce. I led her to the Lord. We had a remarriage ceremony right there. They weren't divorced, but we prayed together and I married them. I had them hold hands in the Lord, and I said, "Thank you, Jesus. Cost $200 to get these two saved, but it's worth the price." God had had us break down for that.

I know a lot of people disagree with me, but I believe in picking up hitchhikers. It might be dangerous, but the worst they could do is kill me, and they'd just be sending me to heaven. But, I haven't heard of a Christian's being killed for witnessing to hitchhikers. Most of us are so poor, they wouldn't want what we have anyway. But if you pick up a hitchhiker once in a while and give him a world witness, you will probably have a lot of good experiences. It will give you a change of pace, and if they don't like what you are saying, they can always get out. They can walk if they don't want to ride with your preaching. It's really a very effective way of witnessing.

My wife, Sherry, once had an experience that shows what can be done even in a dangerous situation. While she was working on the street, some guys grabbed her and put her in a car and took her to Santa Monica beach. They were going to rape her, but she kept preaching to them, so they changed their minds. They took her back to the Strip and told her to get out. She said, "I'm not getting out till we have prayer!" I'll tell you the best protection you can have is a good sermon. It'll take the whole urge of evilness out of someone who's going to do something wrong to you. Just keep spouting out the gospel. Who wants to bother some fanatic who's preaching to them?

You Can Bank on It

Be a witness to the professional people that you deal with. For instance, it's easy to leave a witness at the bank. I've found they'll start getting excited when they see you coming if you've always got a tract hidden among your money. You may have three checks and then a tract, then four more checks. When the teller gets to the tract, you laugh and say, "Well, I did it again." The next time you're in, put the tract in a different place — in the coin bag, in your savings deposit book, etc. She'll never know where it's going to turn up. Sometimes they can't keep a long conversation going because they've got to keep their jobs and the lines have to move along so you have to keep this light. You may say, "I'm still trusting you are going to read that thing and give your heart to Jesus." It's a free atmosphere for witnessing. While they're processing your deposit, you can stand there sharing about Jesus Christ, or about something that has happened in your life in a friendly way.

If you're doing this on a regular basis, it is good to have your name and phone number on the tract. And if the person seems interested, you can say, "If you'd like, I'd be glad for you to give me a jingle on the phone." Or, "If you'd like to talk about it the next time I come in, let me know. I would love to buy you a cup of coffee on your afternoon break or after work." Always make yourself available.

Taking the Doctor's Pulse

Don't neglect your natural relationships with doctors, dentists, pharmacists, etc. You shouldn't feel inferior because you haven't had as much education as some of these people. There are people who say, "I didn't finish school so how can I witness to a guy who knows all the parts of the body?" Well, a person can have a lot of knowledge in one area and still be totally ignorant in another. He may be knowledgeable in his field and doing a good job, and yet not know about Jesus and the Word. Just because someone has an education that exceeds yours, don't be afraid to witness to him. He needs the Lord. I've witnessed to Presidential candidates. In 1972, I witnessed to all the candidates. Then again in 1976, I was entered in a presidential primary and witnessed to most of them again. I found that the people who wanted to run the country didn't know their right hand from their left when it came to spiritual things. I'm not saying that these men are dumb; they're wise, sharp in their field. But they don't have an understanding of how to know Jesus Christ or what spiritual life is all about.

I found a very pleasant way to witness to your doctor. Let's say you are going in for a physical check-up. You can easily compare your physical need with the doctor's own spiritual need. He needs to have the heavenly Doctor give him a check-up.

I remember one time when I came back from Africa my mother wanted me to have a physical exam. She thought I had worms and lice and everything else since I was coming back from a foreign land. When my mother tells me to do something, I do it. Mama is still Mama. So I went down to her country doctor and he tapped and bumped and looked. After he had done a heart analysis, I asked, "Am I alive?" And he said, "You sure are. You are in good shape."

Now, all the while he had been tapping and probing I had been talking about my ministry. He was very interested. Of course, I was actually preaching to him in the third person all along. Then all of a sudden I made it personal by asking, "Doctor, how's *your* heart?" He knew right away what I was talking about. He turned around and he sat down on the examining table. Then he said, "Now, I'm the patient and you're the doctor. I don't know the purpose of life. I see babies born, but I don't know where they're coming from. I see people dying, and I don't know where they're going. Can you help me?" I shared Christ with him and in a little while the nurse came in and nodded her head to remind him of his work. But we kept going through the Scriptures. Later, the nurse came back in, coughed a little and said, "Doctor you've got other patients." He answered, "Please send them to the other doctor. I have got to get this straight. I'm closed until all this is worked out." I sat there and shared with him for a long time about Christ. Finally we knelt on our knees and he invited Jesus to come into his life and be his Savior. Afterwards, he said, "Now I know what people are all about. I understand where they come from and where they are going."

My mother had been going to that doctor for years, but you know she had never asked him to give his heart to Jesus. He knew my mother went to church and my dad went to church. He knew everything about them. He loved them, because they were honest, good people. They could easily have led him to Christ. He had been waiting all these years to be saved. You, too, may have a reputation in your community for being good and honest and dependable. But if you're not sharing with people how they can be saved, your reputation is not helping them to find Jesus.

Your Neighborhood Is Special

There's no other neighborhood in the world quite like yours. I've given you a few ideas of what has worked in other communities, but you have to be creative. Look for the best opportunities available in your particular neighborhood. I'm sure you will find that they are all around you.

5

Jesus Goes Door to Door

It All Started in the New Testament

All sorts of organizations build their success on going door-to-door. But this technique is not the discovery of modern businessmen and cult leaders. It was a major means of evangelism in the early church. I believe that we have the strongest possible New Testament basis for house-to-house sharing of the gospel. In Acts 5:42 we read that "daily in the temple and house to house they ceased not to preach and teach in the name of Jesus." Several other times in the book of Acts it is implied that houses were the center of both outreach and fellowship. Sharing Christ with people in their homes has always been a most effective means of witnessing.

And I believe that if we faithfully witnessed house to house in our neighborhoods then there would be little need of the kind of street evangelism I do. It's in the neighborhood that children can be reached. If you early lead a child in the way he or she should go, you will never have to drag him out of a gutter somewhere. My ministry is to try to reclaim those who should have been won in their neighborhoods. I'm just running a rescue shop at the door of hell and grabbing people before they are actually destroyed. It's much better to reach them before they start on the road to ruin.

Don't Knock Door Knocking

When I was attending college in Mississippi, I felt the call of God to go to Anaconda, Montana, to start a church. I was sponsored as an intern from the college. The plan was to go around in a certain neighborhood and see if there was a prospect of having a church there. I followed the instructions that they gave me. We had little prospect cards and we knocked on every door. I didn't care to do it the way they told us to but I followed their instructions anyway. I knocked at the door and asked, "Are you interested in starting a Southern Baptist Church?" Can you imagine? A Southern Baptist Church in Anaconda, Montana, way up north. No, no, no. All day, in the evening, No, no, no. After a week of hearing No, no, no, the area missionary called and wanted to send me somewhere else. He decided there was no prospect of a church there.

I protested, "But we didn't ask the people if they were saved. Most of them were lost. They aren't interested in a Southern Baptist Church in the north. And most of them don't know what Baptists believe. The people need Jesus, and I would like to go back and go door-to-door telling them about Jesus." The area missionary said, "Well, our work isn't based on one week's analysis. If you want to go, Blessitt, go."

I didn't have any money. I had already come a couple of thousand miles and I was broke. I went to a hotel and said, "I don't have any money, but I'll sleep in the basement and pay you at the end of the month. Anything." They moved some old mops and stuff out of a small room and they put a bunk bed in it. That's where I slept for a dollar a day.

One night I laid down on the floor and prayed through the night, and God gave me this plan. God told me to just knock on as many doors as I could, go all day long, go through the night. He showed me that if I would knock on enough doors and ask enough people to receive Jesus and tell them how to be saved, I would have results. If I would go enough hours to enough doors, sooner or later someone would be saved. And then I just had to keep doing it until a ministry got started in Anaconda. I prayed through the night, lying on the floor, crying and praising God.

The next morning when I walked out the door of the hotel, the guy at the desk asked me, "Are you the guy who's living in that old storage room?" I said, "Yeah," and he said, "Well, you just ran away one of our customers. A prostitute works in the room next to you, and she said that she came in and heard you praying. She pulled her chair up against the wall and listened. You were praying for God to save the sinners. And you said you were going after sinners all day and all night. So she came out and said, 'I'm checking out. I don't want to be in town with that guy.' And she's gone."

Then I started looking for a building. I found an old Salvation Army building that had just become vacant. So I was able to rent a whole church building, piano, organ and everything. I went down in the bar and began witnessing to the guys. They started out laughing at me, but a big guy said, "Leave him alone; I want to hear what he's saying." Later he accepted Christ. In a short time, the Lord had given me a plan of evangelism, a place to stay, a building for ministry and a deeply interested person.

I started going door to door. I'd knock on the door, put on the biggest grin I had, and say, "Hi, I'm Arthur Blessitt. I'm a Christian and I'd like to talk to you about Jesus Christ." People might invite me in or they might slam the door. We found a lot of people interested and led them to Jesus Christ. We organized a church within less than two months. I stayed until they got a full-time pastor and then went back to college. That church is still going, just because I knocked on doors and asked people about their relationship with Jesus Christ.

If They Think You're Pushing a Cult

Most of the people you'll be meeting when you're going door-to-door are not likely to be interested in your church. They're interested in their relationship with God and that's the point you have to stick to.

Many of these people have been hit by Jehovah's Witnesses, by the Hare Krishnas, by Mormons, by Scientology, by everything else going, and when you come to their door, they'll think you're another one of those cults. But don't worry about that. I'd rather be mistaken for something that I'm not than never to be mistaken for anything. Stepping out involves the risk of being misunderstood. I'm not going to let the devil have the world without a fight. He can't have the neighborhood just because some people aren't doing it right. He can't have Hollywood or your neighborhood sin spot just because he got there first. We're going to give him a run for his money. He can't have your neighborhood if you don't let him have it. If you go out into your neighborhood, house-to-house, sharing the good news of Jesus Christ, you may be mistaken at times, but you will never go unnoticed. You'll attract attention to the gospel.

Let Them Know Who You Are

I would suggest that if you are a pastor or another representative of a local church, tell them who you are when you go door-to-door. Now, that doesn't mean you have to get into a strong denominational promotion, but if you're the Baptist pastor or the Catholic priest, you should share it. Then if the person says, "Well, I don't like Baptists," you can say, "I didn't come to talk about Baptists anyway. I'd like to talk to you about your relationship with Christ." Or, if they say, "I don't like Catholics worshiping the Pope," you can say, "Well, I'm not talking about the Pope; let me share with you about Jesus." The value of identifying yourself is that many people will respect your position in the community, or the reputation of your church. If you try to avoid the issue, people think you're trying to mislead them.

If you're not representing any local church, you can say something like this: "My name's Arthur Blessitt, and I'm a Christian in this neighborhood. My friends and I are sharing

Jesus Christ door-to-door throughout the community. We just thought we'd drop by and share with you for a few moments about Jesus Christ."

I find that that's an easy and simple approach. If they ask if you are from a church, you may say, "Well, I'm with the Street University and we're having classes up at such-and-such church." If you feel they're leery about that sort of thing, you might just say, "I'm from Oklahoma, and we're here sharing Jesus Christ door-to-door. What's your relationship with Jesus? Do you know Christ as your Savior?"

Don't Lose Sight of Your Main Purpose

If you are going out from your own church, I would say that you should certainly end up inviting them to come to one of your meetings. There's nothing wrong with that. But, your main interest is to lead the person to Christ. Your second goal may be to invite them into the fellowship, but don't lose sight of your main purpose.

Sometimes people will visit and visit and never get around to asking those they are visiting what their relationship with Jesus is. They hem and haw all around, dropping in little tidbits about God and about the church but they never zero in on the person's salvation. Remember that you're there on God's business and you need to stick to God's business.

If you let the conversation center on the church instead of on the person's spiritual life, you're sure to end up talking about all the problems churches have. He may say, "Boy, some of these churches are messed up." Don't argue with him and don't agree with him. Just share with him about Jesus Christ and about the Bible.

People's past experiences with churches may keep them from being open to yours. You may pray with someone who gives his heart to Jesus. You're so happy that you say, "Praise the Lord, come to the church with me on Sunday." They may respond, "I don't believe in going to church.

That place is a rip-off." And, you might look at him and say, "Gee, you gave your heart to Jesus." "Yeah, but all the church does is ask for money. I don't want to give my money to those hypocrites."

You may feel that he must not really have been saved. But he sincerely prayed; he really invited Christ into his heart. He's just gotten a false idea of what the church is all about. So you may want to say, "Well, I'd love you to come along with me if you'd like to visit." But instead say, "Listen, next Monday night, would it be alright if I came back and we had a Bible study here at your house so I can share more with you?" "Yeah, yeah." If he says no, make another date. "What night can I come back and share with you?" Get him involved in a Bible study. Go back and start teaching him, and soon he'll follow you right in to your church. When you start teaching people the Word, they'll follow you right to where you're getting the food. You'll bring them into your fellowship in time, so don't worry if they don't instantly rush to your church.

Before the Door Slams

People feel very defensive when a stranger comes to their door. Therefore, I suggest that after you knock on the door or punch the buzzer, you take a step back from the door. It's best not to be standing right in the doorway, because it scares them a little. Sometimes a lady jumps back, thinking you're a burglar or you're going to cause some other trouble. If you're standing back at a comfortable distance, it's more relaxing for the person who opens the door. They're more likely to let you share with them.

If the person answers your introductory remarks by saying, "I'm really not interested; I'd rather not talk to you," don't go without leaving some kind of witness. Give them a tract or some stickers, and say, "Here's something you can read right here in the privacy of your home. It will show you how you can take Jesus Christ as your Saviour, how you can invite Him into your heart." Many times as they're closing the door, you can give them the way of salvation in simple terms by describing the literature. They may even ask you, "What do you mean, you can know Jesus Christ will be your Savior?" And the door will be open again. Many times I've just talked for quite a while with people while I was in the process of leaving.

Many people will invite you into their house. If they don't invite me in, then generally I'll just stand there at the door and share with them. Sometimes, I may ask them, "May I come in and sit down and share with you, okay?" But this is not always wise, especially if there's a lady home alone and you're a man. She may feel intimidated. She doesn't know for sure whether she can trust you. So, it is probably best to just stand there at the door and share with her.

What Do You Say?

Let's suppose you've gotten a good reception and you're sitting in someone's living room. Feel free to make some "small talk." Show an interest in their family and their work. Quite often people will say, "Can I get you a cup of coffee or a cold drink?" If I'm thirsty, I say yes, and if I'm not, I say no. I don't feel I'm under obligation just because it's offered.

Now, all the while I'm sitting there I've got my Bible in my hand. I think it's good to go out visiting with your Bible so there is no disguise as to what you're up to. People are less afraid to let you in the house if they see you've got a well-worn Bible, and it indicates that you're for real. That Bible in your hand does one more thing: it reminds you what you're there for.

So don't waste too much time before you get to the point. You can say, "Listen, I've come here to really share with you about your relationship with Jesus Christ. Jesus Christ came into my heart and He changed my life so I'd like to talk with you about your relationship with God. If you were to die today, do you have the assurance you'd go to heaven?" He may answer, "Well, I used to attend church regularly, I'm really kind of a religious man. But we just moved down here." "Well, that's wonderful. You've got a background in the Bible. But I want to ask you personally, right now, do you know for sure that Jesus Christ is your Savior?" "Well, I hope so." "Listen, let me show you how you can know for sure about your relationship with Jesus. Look at this verse with me." And you go right into the Bible plan of salvation.

Follow-up Means Finishing What You Start

I would suggest that when you are evangelizing your neighborhood, whether as part of a church outreach or as an individual, it is good to carry a pocketful of index cards so that you can make a notation as to what the response was at a given house. Then you can block off the area and note that there are so many people along here, at this address and this one and this one, who gave their hearts to Christ. Then you can plan to come back to bring a Bible to them or to help them get started in Bible study. Another time if you'll do this systematically, then you can cover your entire neighborhood, and you will have a good feeling of accomplishment, knowing that every house within a mile of your home or your church has been given the gospel of Jesus Christ. You can feel peace with God as you think of facing Him on the day of judgment.

Any place where you think a follow-up visit may help should be recorded on a card. Give these cards to your pastor or whoever is in charge of the outreach program. Then a continuing follow-up can be developed for that neighborhood.

When people open up to you in their homes, they will often reveal some of the problems they are going through or some other concerns they have. They may be concerned about getting married, they may be having marital problems, they may be interested in church membership. Some of these problems would require a course in Christian counseling. Then note this on your index card, so your pastor, or someone who's been trained and would have an idea of how to advise people, can make the follow-up visit. In your assignments, try to determine what the need is and match a visitor to that need.

The Dynamite of Home Bible Studies

A very effective means of neighborhood evangelism is the development of home Bible study groups. You find a home where the people let you come in for a Bible study, and then have them invite their neighbors. This kind of group will grow and grow and grow just from the natural contacts people have.

I found this to be very effective when I was in the U.S. Presidential campaign in New Hampshire in 1976. We would organize what we'd call a "home meeting." We had them all over New Hampshire. One person would invite a group of friends to come to their house to meet me. They knew in advance that I'd speak for 15 minutes about my relationship with Jesus Christ. Then, I would have prayer and a time of questions and answers. Do you know, we had more of those home meetings than we could book, day after day after day. It didn't matter whether the person who arranged the home meeting was saved or lost as long as he would invite me in to meet me and allow me to talk about both the Presidency and Jesus Christ.

The smallest home meeting we had drew ten people, and the largest just over 100. I had them morning, afternoon and evening of nearly every day and had only one meeting where no one was saved. I was running for President. You can imagine why I didn't win, praise the Lord. But maybe we *did* win. We saw definite commitments by over 800 people who were saved in New Hampshire. I still get letters from New Hampshire. A guy just wrote to me who used to be a race car driver. He's now in seminary. He accepted Christ in one of those home meetings. Some of these groups are *still* continuing in connection with a local fellowship.

I would love to see a church have an evangelism crusade centered around home Bible studies. They may invite an evangelist or just use the pastor. The meetings will be set up by all the church members inviting people in their neighborhoods to meet the pastor or evangelist. They should be told that he's going to speak for a while about Jesus Christ and then they can ask him questions. If they know they can ask questions, they'll be more likely to come. Just do that for a week, morning, noon, night, and then have a Sunday rally. They'll come, because you've built the interest throughout the week.

Prospecting for Prospects

Prospect witnessing is basically a local church ministry and outreach. Someone has visited your church and has filled out a visitor's card. Or someone has been in contact with the pastor about some problem. You can count on them to be somewhat open because of these previous contacts.

You can divide these prospects into two groups: those who are already Christians and need some kind of Christian ministry or counseling, and those who have not yet received Christ. Some people can make the first type of visit best, and others are better equipped for straight evangelism.

Now, it is very important that you identify yourself when you go to the prospect's home because some of them may not be interested in talking to you otherwise. They've been to your church and they may know the pastor, but they don't know anyone else. But if you identify yourself with the church, you'll receive a warmer response.

I refuse to visit with a prospect if someone gives me the name and says, "Don't tell them how you got it." A lady may say, "Will you drop in on my husband, but don't tell him I told you to do it." Then I just say, "Well, you either give me permission to use your name or you do the witnessing yourself. Otherwise, I might be forced to lie and I might disgrace the church. He'll say, "Where did you get my name?" "Well, you know, somebody recommended you," and the guy starts thinking, "What have I done?" It's better to be able to say, "Your wife is with the church and she asked me to drop by and meet you sometime, so here I am." Boy, if the wife doesn't have that much of a relationship with her husband, things are already in bad shape. She needs some counseling herself.

In the case of prospect visits, I definitely feel you should invite yourself in. You might say, "May I please come in and meet you and visit in your home a moment?" There is reason to be a little more personal in this kind of visit than in cold contacts door-to-door. You've identified yourself as coming from the church where he's already had some positive contact, so you can be a bit more aggressive. Be positive and expect a positive response. "I'd like to come in and talk with you just a moment. I'm sure you don't mind." It's hard for a person to say no to an approach like that.

Adapt to Circumstances

You have a picture in your mind of what a visit is going to be like, but the situation may turn out to be completely different than you thought. The people you visit may be involved in something intriguing. You watch what they're doing. A guy may be gardening, and you can see he's working hard at it. You can just kind of follow along, talking about his tomato plants and bringing in the gospel however you can. You may say, "Isn't it wonderful, you see those seeds planted and then they spring to life and come up. It reminds me of a new birth, of how we can be born again spiritually. Have you ever been born again?" "I don't even know the term. What do you mean by that?" And you can share with him how he can have a relationship with Christ, while the guy is still working along in his little garden. After you've gone through the way of salvation with him, you can turn to him and say, "Listen, how about us having a word of prayer right here, right now? Just let Jesus come into your heart. I'd love to pray for you." All the time the guy has been working away and you've been sharing. Now you simply stop and he prays to trust Jesus. It's just beautiful. The opportunity is right there for you, but you have to adapt to the circumstances.

You may come up to another house, and the guy's in the backyard revving up his big old Harley Davidson. You look at his bike. You may not know a Harley Davidson from a VW but you can tell he's all excited about it. And you can say, "I bet that thing really goes, doesn't it?" He says, "Yeah, it really does, really fast." And you can say, "Listen, if you were on that thing going 90 miles an hour, and it didn't make it around a curve and hit a light pole, where do you think you'd spend eternity?" The guy will look up, startled, so you give him a big old grin and say, "Listen, do you know Jesus in your life? What's your relationship with God?" You're right on with him. You've taken that thing he's interested in and related it to his spiritual need.

You don't have to feel bound to witnessing the same way in every circumstance. But, on the other hand, you do need to get to the point pretty quickly. Otherwise, you'll spend all your time talking about gardening or motorcycles.

Don't Give Up on Those Security Apartments

Security apartments are becoming more and more common. You can't get into them unless you push a button and talk over an intercom. And there are *NO SOLICITING* signs posted all around. Boy, I don't worry about the *NO*

SOLICITING signs because I'm not soliciting. I'm *giving away* the gospel. But if they order you out, you generally have to go.

The key to working in a security apartment is to have a friend inside. If you know someone who lives in the apartment and he will go with you, then that's great. You just go in. You've got a friend there! You punch the buzzer and walk in. You can do a lot of creative things if you have that inside contact. I've found it very effective to have a party or a reception in the recreation room. You have your friend who lives in the apartment building reserve it for one night or one afternoon, and then have them go around putting notes under everyone's door: *Alice Brown in room 305 is inviting you to a hamburger fry and 'Meet My Pastor Party' (or testimony party or something like that) at the recreation room. Everybody is welcome.*" Put the notice on the bulletin board as well, and you'll have a good crowd.

If you're living in a family apartment complex, you can have a party for all the kids. Give them free hotdogs or hamburgers, and they'll be swarming around you.

I know a number of places that have services every week in the recreation room, through one of the people in the apartment. Others have a Bible study in the recreation room. So if you are creative, you will find a way to get in there even though going door-to-door is impossible.

Phone Book Witnessing

When a neighborhood seems closed to door-to-door evangelism, don't give up on it. There are two ways you can get into those houses besides the front door: through the telephone and through the mailbox.

After I left seminary, I went to work in Elko, Nevada, because the Lord burdened my wife, Sherry, and me to go there. We began witnessing in bars and casinos, and we had a few converts. We tried going door-to-door. We also called every name in the phone book from A to Z. Some were saved on the phone; we made appointments to visit others at their homes.

Your Neighborhood Mission Field

If you faithfully work in your neighborhood, you'll see results. We need to confront our neighborhoods with Jesus Christ. They all need to hear about Him—the people in the apartment where you live, the people who live next door to you, the people you work with, the people you meet in stores, supermarkets, shopping malls. God has put this ready-made mission field near you so that you can share Jesus with every person.

6

Jesus Goes Where the People Are

Your witnessing should start in your neighborhood, but it shouldn't end there. Wherever the Lord gives you the opportunity to go, there will be needy people. So keep alert.

Coffee, Tea, or Thee?

People who are traveling are open to a gospel witness. Paul knew that, because he witnessed to people on a ship (Acts 27).

I've only taken one boat cruise, but I had a great time on that ship. It was sailing from the Canary Islands to Sierra Leone, West Africa. I was going to start carrying the cross from Sierra Leone to the Indian Ocean, 4,500 miles across Africa. It was just terrific right from the beginning. Even before I got on the ship, I had the chance to witness. They put a hoist on the cross. They wouldn't let me carry it on the gangplank because of Longshoremen's union regulations. They had the cross way up in the sky and were carrying it over and putting it in the hold of the ship. Everybody around the boat began saying, "He's the one with that big cross down there." And all sorts of witnessing opportunities opened up to me.

I don't get to ride boats much, but I do airplanes. One day I was on a plane and the stewardess was giving us the information that in case of an emergency the gismo will drop down from above you and you're supposed to grab it. And they always say, "Breathe normally." Can you imagine breathing normally if they tell you the plane's going down? Breathe normally.

Well, we were ready to take off and the stewardess began her little pitch. She said, "In case of an emergency . . ." And I hollered, "Pray!" She came back when she was finished and said, "Would you mind restraining yourself?" I said, "If this thing starts down, we're going to need more than oxygen; we're going to need the Lord."

I learned what *not* to do on one airplane. I was witnessing to the stewardesses and I said, "Let me ask you this. If this plane would explode, where would you spend eternity?" That ruined my witness. They were shook up. They said, "You can be arrested for saying things like that." I said, "I didn't say I was going to blow it up." "You're not even supposed to talk that way." I tried to witness more after that but they just looked at me suspiciously. I went up later, and they were looking at my attache' case. They eyeballed me the whole trip.

One night I was asleep on a plane, and the stewardess shook me. She was standing there with her little chart in her hand, and she said, "What is your final destination, sir?" Well, I couldn't pass that one up. I told her what it was!

Room Service for Jesus

If you travel a lot, hotels and motels can be one of your most effective places to witness. I love to check into a hotel. It's almost worth the money just to get to fill out the registration card. When they hand me the card, I fill it out my own way. I put down: *name,* Arthur Blessitt; *address,* heaven; *phone no.* J E S U S, call any time; *occupation,* preacher of the love of Jesus Christ for the salvation of people everywhere; *representing,* the Lord Jesus Christ. Then I hand it to the clerk and watch. He'll give you a funny look, but if you've got the cash they'll take you regardless of what you put down. But you can have a world of fun just being able to share Christ.

When I pay for the room, I hand the clerk the money or credit card with a tract on top. They'll always take it when you do it that way, but they might not if you tried to hand them a tract alone. They want that money, and they'll endure the witness if they can get the cash for it.

A Quick Witness at a Fast Foods Place

You can usually circulate freely in a fast foods restaurant like McDonald's. As long as you're quiet and don't interfere with their business they won't bother you. There are so many Christians who trade at a particular McDonald's that they don't say anything because they want the church's business. Of course, if they were to say, "No, you can't witness here," you would have to stop because that is really private property. Usually, however, you can go quietly from table to table and share with people.

You also run into some of the same kind of lonely people you meet in bars. They often sit in a fast foods restaurant and wish for someone to talk to. I remember once when I was just there to eat. I wasn't prepared to witness, had no stickers or tracts. I was reading the newspaper, when a guy rushed up to me and asked, "Who won?" I said, "Jesus did." The guy looked at me. Then he said, "No, no, who won the *ballgame?*" And I said, "Ballgames don't turn me on, but Jesus does." He said, "You're weird," and he went walking out. But I felt like the normal one.

You know, I've found that some people have a handicap that only gives them trouble when you mention their relationship with Jesus. A lot of times when you ask someone, "Have you received Christ as your Lord?" they start coughing. Did you ever notice that? Or, their handicap may be that they're hard of hearing. You'll ask them, "Are you saved?" And they'll say, "What?" They always seem to have some kind of handicap when it comes to talking about Christ.

The Main Course is Not on the Menu

You can also witness in the classier sit-down restaurants. After I'm done with the menu, I always put a tract inside of it. The waitress doesn't usually open it again; she just passes your tract right on to the next person.

If they have a "Today's Special," I try to stick the tract right there. The tract's entitled "The Big Question." They'll think it's a surprise dinner, like a sneak preview. "Oh, today's special, the Big Question. That sounds good." They open it up: "If you die this minute, do you have the assurance . . ." They've never had a meal like that before.

Don't neglect the opportunity to witness to your waitress. When she gives you the menu, say, "Thanks so much, that's a lovely menu. Let me give you another lovely menu that shares about the spiritual food you can have." They may become so under conviction that they'll spill water or soup on you. They may mix up your order, but bear with them. You can't go in and witness and then scream and holler if they give you the wrong thing. If you present yourself as a Christian, you've got to maintain that witness. If they burn your hamburger, say, "Praise the Lord, the hamburger's burnt. I don't think I'm going to be able to eat it, but if you don't mind I sure could use another one that's not quite so crispy." If it seems to be a bother, say, "Praise the Lord, I'll just fast this meal." But be nice about it, whatever you do. Don't go in and witness and then ruin your testimony by getting all stirred up over something.

I also like to work on the napkin rack. That's one of my favorites. You flip back through a few napkins, stick a tract in and push the napkins back. Folks will be eating and reach for a napkin and just kind of wipe on the Word. Or you can stick a sticker on the bottom of a ketchup bottle. When people shake it upside down — good gracious, "Turn on to Jesus." I don't stick them on the plates or silverware, because then the dishwasher has to peel them off.

Hi There, Sports Fans

I've had some interesting experiences preaching or witnessing at sports events. One time I felt a strong burden to preach at a wrestling match. I didn't tell anyone about it, because they would have thought I was crazy. I just went down and talked to the guy who ran the wrestling arena. I'd never met him before. I just went up to him and I said, "I'm Arthur Blessitt, and the Lord's laid it on my heart to preach during the wrestling match." He said, "I've never heard of such a thing." I admitted I hadn't either.

He said he'd have to think about it. I said, "You think about it, and I'll pray." I bowed my head right there. He was on one side of the bar, and I was on the other. When I'd finished praying, I looked up and he was still standing there looking at me. I said, "God told me yes; what did He tell you?" and he said, "When are you coming?" He put an ad in the newspaper listing all the wrestlers. So-and-so vs. so-and-so, right down the ad, and at the bottom was my name. He didn't list me as fighting anybody.

Well, I went. You know how it is with wrestling matches, a whole bunch of wild fans. Have you ever watched that stuff on television? I don't like it. Some big guy is on the bottom and the crowd's hollering, "Kill him, kill him, kill him!" We had planned to have gospel singing before the match started but the owner changed his mind about that part of it. He said he'd just let me preach afterward. I said, "It won't work because everybody will leave after the match. As soon as that last fight's over, everyone will be dashing for the door." He said, "I know it." I stood there a second, my mind just flying. Then I said, "O.K., I'll take you up on it." He asked, "What are you going to do?" I said, "You watch; the crowd won't leave. They'll stay."

He kept watching me during the match. These big guys were wrestling, picking each other up, twisting arms and legs. The people were yelling, "Kill him!" And I was sitting there praying, "Lord save them all tonight, save them all."

Finally it was the last match, and a big guy was down on his back. The referee would count, "One, two, . . " but the guy would wiggle his shoulder. Then, he'd be down again. "One, two, . . ." Finally I said, "Lord, hold him down." Up went the other shoulder. "One, two, three . . ." and it was over.

The crowd was standing there screaming. I jumped into the ring and I grabbed the microphone. I said, "Now ladies and gentlemen, the main event!" They all grabbed their programs and checked them out. They started looking around, then they sat down. I didn't say a word, I just stood there. They all became quiet, and I said, "The main event tonight, God vs. the devil." They still listened. Now I knew this wouldn't hold them long so I made as fast a run as I could from Genesis to Revelation in five short minutes. I gave the invitation and people came forward to give their lives to Jesus. I stayed there counseling people for a while afterward.

A Day at the Races

I had been walking with my cross 4,000 miles across Africa, and I happened to arrive in Nairobi the day of the East African Safari Road Race. That was quite a reception. There were hundreds of thousands of people. They were lined up all along the route.

Well, I dragged my cross right down that road while the people were waiting for the race. I had an interpreter and I preached every block or so. I'd preach for about three or four minutes, no long sermon, and just invite the people to pray. I wanted to expose the whole crowd to the gospel. The soldiers and police didn't bother me at all. I preached that day to tens of thousands of people. Every block I'd stand the cross up and share about Jesus Christ dying on His cross, and how He was resurrected, and He's alive today. I told them they could repent of their sins and ask Him to come into their hearts and be their Savior. Then I'd give them a prayer to pray, and move down the next block. We could have stayed away from that crowd and had no witness at all. But God had let that crowd gather, so I decided to get out in the middle of it and go for Jesus. I was ready to stop as soon as the army or police told me to, but they never did.

Good Vibes at a Rock Festival

Sports events attract crowds, and so do rock festivals. Wherever the people are gathered, that's where you should be sharing Jesus. I remember right after the Woodstock Rock Festival took place, I prayed and said, "Lord, when the next rock festival occurs, I want to preach on that stage. I don't know where the next one's taking place, but wherever it is, I'll get in there and by Your grace, I'll preach."

I had been sick; I had had several strokes back in the late 60's. The doctors wanted to keep me in the hospital but I wanted to keep an engagement in West Palm Beach. I was awfully sick. I lay across a few seats on the airplane. Then I canceled all my meetings except the one open-air rally. I preached there, flew back to L.A. and spent some time recovering.

A while later I received a phone call from West Palm Beach. The guy said, "I'm the promoter of the West Palm Beach International Rock Festival—the biggest rock festival since Woodstock. We've got Janis Joplin, Jimi Hendrix, The Rolling Stones, Sly and the Family Stone—all the heavyweights of the rock business, and I want you to come and preach during the festival." I asked, "Why do you want me to come and preach?" He said, "Well, my wife was converted at your open-air rally down here and she talked with you after it was over. You gave her your card, and she's been on my back ever since. She said, 'You've got all these dope-taking freaks coming in here; you need a preacher to preach to them. If you let the guy on the stage, he'll do the kids some good.' " He said they were having opposition from Christians who didn't want a rock festival there, so having a preacher on the program would help them.

I spent a whole week there. I preached on stage five times. *Time* magazine did a story in their December, 1969 edition, and we had 30,000 kids at our Easter sunrise service. I witnessed to Janis Joplin, Jimi Hendrix, and just about every group there. We set up a Jesus tent and did all kinds of ministry. All this happened just because I responded and was faithful even when my physical body was totally wiped out and dilapidated. God sent me to that open-air rally, saved that woman, and brought us together again.

That was a new kind of Christian witness. It started a trend, and there hasn't been a major event since where the gospel of Jesus Christ hasn't been preached. At all the motorcycle races, pop festivals, the Rose Parade, etc., Christians have been blitzing people with the gospel. It all started with that festival in West Palm Beach.

Sand in Your Sandals for Jesus

I've found that people on the beach are *very* responsive. Often they are more open than they would be fully dressed and walking down the street. Sometimes they're bored and would like someone to talk with while they're soaking up the sun.

The key thing about beach witnessing is to be casual. Be casual in your dress. It's kind of silly for you to be out witnessing in your Sunday best, when everyone else is in a bathing suit. People will think, "Here come the Christians," and they'll be turned off before you get to them. Your approach should also be casual. Just ease around from person to person with a tract and a friendly word. There should be an air of quiet excitement about you, but high pressure techniques don't work on the beach. And, also, remember to be considerate.

If a person's sleeping, don't wake him. Be courteous, rather than obnoxious. And don't litter the beach. If a person throws down a tract you've given him, pick it up. You don't like to see newspapers and tin cans littering the beach, so you can understand how unbelievers feel about tracts laying all over the place. Littering is not a great kind of witnessing.

What do you say to a person you approach on the beach? I find it's natural to kneel down next to a person, so you're more on his level. Then you can hand him a tract and say, "Hey, can I turn you on to something to read?" You'll really attract his attention if you say, "Listen, I'd like to turn you on to some reds." Of course, you're all ready to give him some little red stickers that say "Turn On To Jesus," and things like that. If the person doesn't want to talk, don't force it. Say, "Thank you; praise the Lord," and go on.

When you work a beach one-on-one you can have amazing results. I have led guys to Christ, walked with them back to their vans and watched while they took all their dope and threw it in the ocean. You can also do effective one-on-one witnessing in parking lots, boardwalks and shop areas along the beach.

A group of Christians can really make an impact through a beach blitz. The Christians can spread all over that beach in one-on-one witnessing. Then they can gather together and begin some informal singing. This will inevitably attract a crowd. When quite a few have gathered around your little circle, the leader of the group can say, "It's good to see so many of you standing around. Let me share with you what Jesus Christ has done for me." Then he should give a brief testimony and invite people to pray to receive Jesus. The other Christians can talk to those who do.

If you feel led to preach on the beach, don't do it where the people are already gathered together. They're there to relax, so your preaching will annoy and antagonize them. Instead, find a clear area, and when you begin to preach, those who are interested will gather around you.

If the beach near you has an amphitheater, why not organize a large beach rally. I've done this on Daytona Beach, and it's amazing how many onlookers have gathered. Thousands of people put their blankets around the amphitheater so they could hear what was going on.

And in Fort Lauderdale, we had excellent results in a one-day beach blitz. All the Christians worked the beach all day in one-on-one witnessing and small praise services. Then at night we preached in clubs near the beach. Many were converted and wanted to be baptized, so at midnight we went back to the beach. I baptized 300 people in the ocean that one night. I was exhausted, but rejoicing, when that day was over.

Adults Only

I don't recommend this kind of ministry for everyone, but I've been able to preach in adult movie theaters.

I was witnessing along the streets of Laconia, New Hampshire, and I noticed that there was only one movie in town, and it was showing a movie rated XXX. I said, "Great prospect." I went in with my Bible, walked up to the ticket counter and started talking to the lady who was also the manager. I was talking to the lady about the Lord, sharing with her about Jesus. Finally, I said, "Well, if you're not going to give your heart to Jesus, you could do the next best thing." She said, "What's that?" I said, "Take this old dirty movie off and put on a good movie," and I grinned in a friendly way. She said, "I can't do that. This is drawing the crowd." "O.K.," I said, "Then at least let me preach during popcorn time." She said, "I've never heard of such a thing, but O.K. When do you want to come?" I said, "Tomorrow night."

So, I went back the next night. And do you know she

had it on the marquee: "XXX The Maid in Sweden; XXX Arthur Blessitt." I looked like I was starring in the movie. I said, "I hope nobody takes a picture." Sure enough, the Laconia newspapers came, because one of the reporters had heard me preach. Arthur Blessitt at the theater tonight? It sounded like a good story.

But it turned out to be quite a funny story. The manager said to me, "As soon as that reel finishes, you can have about four minutes of preaching time, and then we put the show back on. When the reel is near the end, I'll let you know, and you can go in." So I stood and talked with her until it was near to the end. Then she turned a big spotlight on the stage and I stepped up.

Now you've gotta be ready to go when you're in a porno show, so I stepped up smiling. They thought I was a live comedian, and that's just what I wanted them to think so that they would listen. I said, "You've been watching this movie, 'The Maid in Sweden.' I want to talk to you about the maid at the well." That's from John 4 in the Bible but they didn't know that. "There was this sexy chick, you know, and she was hooking around town and she was shacked up with this dude." They were listening, grinning, ready for me to go into the punch-line. I built it up, saying, "There was a man, who came up to where she was standing and said, 'Give me a drink.' " I finally dropped it on them: "And *Jesus* said to her . . ." Then I started preaching.

One by one people started getting up. They all left except seven and they didn't come back. No popcorn, they just went out the door. The lady was dying laughing. I didn't abuse my time. I kept to the four minutes. If you ever are on a program like that, where someone gives you four minutes, don't go over four minutes. Don't just wind up and keep preaching all day. Honor their time and your agreement with them.

Afterwards, the lady manager said, "Do you know why those others didn't leave?" I knew that two of them were with me, but the other five were strangers. She said, "Those are the bank president and four of his friends. They saw the news photographers and they're afraid to leave.

You've got to adapt to circumstances. We had an outreach building near Times Square, New York, for about three months in 1971. It was right between two topless nightclubs. Now if you've been in New York City, you'll know what I'm talking about. They have little peep holes in the front door or windows. You can peek in and that's how they get you interested so that you'll go in.

Here was our building right between two of them. What were we going to do, put up a "Jesus Saves" banner? There would be nothing wrong with that, but I thought that in New York people wouldn't even notice it. Just more of those fanatical Christians. So here's what we did. We covered the front windows with red paper and put a big sign in front saying, *TOTALLY NAKED, TOTALLY NAKED!* And then we put a peep hole under the sign. When people looked in, all they saw was a mirror reflecting their own face, and under it a sign that said, *NAKED YOU STAND BEFORE GOD.* Then there were a few Scripture verses printed beneath it.

That may seem like a strange idea to you, but I believe in battling the devil in his territory. And our store front was a sensation. We had people lined up down the sidewalk to look in. Of course, a thing like that only attracts people for a little while, but you have to use every means you can to get a hearing for the gospel.

7

Starting Your Own Outreach Center

Do You Have to Start with a Building?

How can you establish an outreach center for Jesus Christ? All you *really* need is the love of Jesus in your heart and a Bible under your arm. That's enough to tear any town up. As a matter of fact, Paul and Peter, when they were causing such havoc for the Lord, didn't even have a New Testament. All they had was the Old Testament. So get the Word of God and go to work.

Some people think it takes a lot of money to get a ministry going for Christ. They say, if I had the money, I'd start to work for the Lord." But really, all you need to do is start sharing Jesus Christ in love on a consistent day-by-day basis, and soon you'll be ministering to so many people that a building may become an asset. By itself, it may become a liability, because once you open a building, you've got to stay there and make sure it's run right.

When we opened His Place back in 1968, I had to stay there almost a solid year. Every night, seven nights a week I was in that building. If I hadn't, others would take it over—drug dealers or street gangs or some other kind of group. None of us knew how to run it. We just had to learn by making mistakes. I had to *be* there. The building kept me off the streets.

Fit the Building to Your Goal in Ministry

I would suggest that you begin your ministry person to

person, and if you can keep from renting a building, do so. But if it seems necessary, be careful to find a building that meets your specific needs. Decide whom you're going to try to reach and the kinds of activities you're going to conduct. If you don't let your program determine the building, the building will determine who comes and who doesn't come and what you're able to do.

On Sunset Strip, we had a building with no chairs, just a spool table and a floor to sit on. We had free coffee and free sandwiches, which guaranteed that we would draw the people who needed something to eat. This approach would not draw on a consistent basis. There's the guy that's riding around in a Jaguar, and of course, he has as much of a need for Jesus as the one who's penniless. But the Jaguar drivers aren't going to come and sit on the floor and eat leftover bagels. But, you see, we were trying to reach the people who were in the street at that time, and we made the building adaptable to the kind of program that would make them feel at home when they came in.

You have to determine whether your ministry is going to be a Christian coffee house or Jesus nightclub or whether it is going to be an evangelistic outreach for those who need Jesus Christ in the area where you're working. You could open a building right now on Hollywood Boulevard and fill it up with Christians, but you wouldn't reach the street people. If you have too many Christians in an outreach center, you'll run off the people who aren't Christians. It's too holy.

Now, don't get me wrong; you can't really be too holy; God wants us to be holy. But if you've got a whole bunch of Christians jammed in there, drinking coffee, hollering "Praise the Lord" all night, the hookers and pimps and dealers will stay away. They'll say, "That's a Jesus freak spot." You need to develop a good solid group of workers who work consistently and know the people who are coming in and out. They get to understand them and be sensitive to them. Then keep the other Christians out. Your workers will be able to witness to everybody who comes into that building night by night, and you'll be effective. But if you let too many Christians come in, they'll drive them off.

Chase Away the Christian Tourists

Let me illustrate. Night after night at His Place we'd have a good group of street people in. Then a church group would come down two or three nights. They were good, wonderful Christians. But they would stand there gaping—"Could you point out to me a saved motorcycle rider? Which one of these girls used to dance in a go-go club?" They stood around there like Christian tourists just staring and saying, "Look at that one, would you." Boy, we found that the attendance would drop off badly for the next several nights. It would take a week to build it back up. Finally, I realized that these outside Christians were really hurting the ministry.

Now, we didn't want to drive away the Christians. So here's how we handled it. A group of Christians would come along. We'd grab them before they got to the back of the building. We'd bring them all into the office and share with them briefly how we operated. We'd show them the tracts we were using and share with them how they could lead someone to Jesus Christ. Then we would send them out in the street and ban them from coming back 'til midnight, when we had our preaching service. We wanted them to spend time working on the streets first. If they stayed in the building, they wouldn't become sensitive to the people.

If you're running this kind of an outreach, you'll have a lot of people who become quite regular. One night one of these regulars may just want to be left alone. Maybe the guy's tired of hassles, hassles, hassles in the street, and he wants to be able to come in, find a little quiet corner and sit down. He may be really spaced out or just sick of people. He just wants to sit down and be peaceful. You've witnessed to him, all the staff has witnessed to him. But this night when he comes in, it's best not to bother him. You say, "Hey, man, how's it going?" "I just want to sit down for a while." You keep your eye on him, and later you may ease down on the floor next to him and say, "What's happening?" "Look, I don't want to talk tonight." He may even do that several nights. One night he'll be ready to talk. You're ready when he is. But just think what it would be like if you had fifty Christians pouring through, and all fifty of them hit him, every night. He wouldn't come back. If you want to hit him, hit him on the streets. You can't get too much witnessing on the street. But in your place of ministry, it's better to control it.

Your particular outreach ministry needs to fit your area. If we were to decide that we should open another His Place in Hollywood, it wouldn't be designed the same as the first one was, because there's a different crowd there now.

Fit the Building to Your Neighborhood

There's a different feel. When His Place became so well known around the world, a lot of people read *Turned On to Jesus* and tried to open a similar place. They tried staying open all night, but in some of those small towns, nobody moves after a certain hour. Some of them turned out to be more effective in the afternoon. You have to analyze your community, analyze the need, analyze the people, and then provide the right ministry.

Maybe you're thinking of having a Christian ministry. There is a need for Christian coffee houses and Christian clubs where church kids and their friends can go for a date and hear some good music. That can be good, too. It's a different situation than an outreach to non-Christians. If that's your goal, then everyone should know it's a Christian place. You shouldn't permit or tolerate a lot of the things you do when you're dealing with people right off the street. You don't want a bunch of 13-, 14-, and 15-year-old girls who are nice and wholesome mixed in on a regular basis with people who are pushing hard drugs and who are rolling others on the street. And you don't have to try to keep them segregated. They will be segregated automatically by the location and style of your ministry.

If you want to use a building to reach an area, its location is very important. One block can make the difference in whether that building is a success or failure. If your building is right in the flow of the foot traffic, they'll come in just because you have a door open. But if you're located one block out of the way, you've got to go out there and round them up by passing out handbills and every other kind of promotion you can think of. If you had to pay rent for a building in a strategic spot and someone offered to give you a building two blocks away, you may do better to turn down the one you could have for nothing in order to be located in the right place.

It's also important that you determine right at the beginning what you want that building to be. You have to decide whether you're starting a church, an evangelistic outreach or a Christian spiritual ministry center. You can't mix them all together. My basic calling is as an evangelist. I make no bones about it. That's what God has called and led me into. So on a daily basis, I put most of my efforts into direct evangelism. I do not baptize all the people I deal with on the streets. I want them to get into a local church, because I am not starting my own church. There are enough churches in the area. When I've been working in other parts of the world and have come into villages and towns where there was no church, I had a different practice. As soon as I was through preaching, I'd appoint someone to be the pastor, teach him what a church is and get him started. But that isn't the need, as far as I see it in Hollywood.

If you feel led that a certain area needs a church, then you should follow that leading. But make sure you start it as a church and let everyone know that's what you're doing. Sometimes people start in evangelism, but they don't keep their priorities straight. So they develop into a church anyway. They win people, teach them the Bible, baptize them, and all of a sudden they have a church. Fine, if that's your call. But if you're called to evangelism, stick to evangelism. If you are an evangelist, other churches will cooperate with your ministry. But if you start a church, the other churches as a whole will not work with you. They won't bring their people down if they think you're going to be taking their members. You become a threat to all the other churches in the neighborhood, and then you won't have a united outreach effort. If you're talking about starting an outreach ministry, it should stay an outreach ministry. Lead your converts into local churches where follow-up is done on a continuing basis.

It's ideal if you can open your ministry with the support of all the local churches. But it doesn't always work that way. There are times when no one seems to want to cooperate with a new ministry, and you have to go out on your own and do it. It's better if the local churches pool resources to underwrite the work and encourage their people to be involved in the outreach. But you may have to start on your own and prove yourself first. They may not be convinced that you're going to follow through on what you've said you're going to do. They want to watch you for a while. But when you're there get out and do it regularly. You'll find there's a lot more support than you had originally thought.

Another thing you need to deal with when you're in this kind of ministry is your own feelings. Don't wear your feelings on your shoulder and become embittered against people who differ with you. Don't become bitter against a church when you share with the pastor and say, "Wow, last night we were out and we led twenty to Jesus . . . God's sweeping up," and the pastor kind of looks at you a little funny. He may have his reasons. He may have run across a lot of overnight wonders who didn't have a solid foundation under what they were doing and disappeared as fast as they had come. Or maybe he's never experienced this kind of thing and doesn't know what to make of it. If you get mad at him and go around badmouthing that church, if you fall into a pattern of criticizing, your own life will be embittered.

God hasn't called those of us who are evangelists to fight against the work of God in the churches. Don't become dogmatic and think that everyone else in the world has got to do things the same way you do. If you ever get that way, then your own ministry will become maladjusted. It would be the easiest thing in the world for me to say, "Just look around. I'm the only one out there. All those other preachers are home in front of their T.V. sets. Everybody ought to be out all night long." That's a self-righteous attitude.

None of us can do anything for the Lord except by His grace and through His strength. I'm working at night on the street and I *still* feel guilty about how little is being done. But I'm not visiting the hospitals, I'm not ministering on a regular basis in the jails, I'm not teaching those precious children. I'm out there running a rescue shot right at the gates of hell, but the Sunday school teacher who's working with children four or five years old is training them so that they'll never get that messed up. I thank the Lord for my Sunday school teachers and for a mother who spent time with me and led me to Jesus as a child and taught me in the way of Christ. As a result, I never did wind up stoned out of my mind somewhere, or in jail for some crime, or drunk and all messed up. It was because they did their jobs.

When They Criticize You

We get all excited about what God's doing in our little part of the body of Jesus, and we don't see anybody else. We want them all to be just like us. Instead, we should realize that the work of God is very big. It's bigger than me, it's bigger than you. The greatest minister among us is only one small part in the overall work of God in people's lives. So get your perspective right, get your balance right. Know what it is that God wants you to do, but don't go around with a chip on your shoulder toward everyone who doesn't understand your ministry.

Walking with the cross has done a lot to mellow me. When you go out and do a thing like that, a lot of people think you're weird, a lot of godly, good people think you're nuts just because they don't understand. I have to think about when I was pastoring in 1964 and 1965. If one of my church members called on the phone and said, "There's some nut out here with a big old cross with a wheel on the end of it, dragging it down the road," I probably would have said, "I'm not even going to go look. I've got too much to do. There are all kinds of nuts in the world." I've learned that the fact that someone doesn't understand what I'm doing when I'm walking down the road with the cross doesn't mean he's not spiritual. What it really means is that he's never had a chance to meet us and get to know the motivation behind it.

So, when you are out ministering in your way and someone doesn't understand you, relax about it. Even if they criticize you ("I don't think you ought to be out there with all these terrible people.") don't become bitter toward them. They've never been out there with you. They've never seen what you've seen. And, of course, you don't see what they see either. You just learn to love them and praise the Lord and say, "Well, pray for me." Keep on doing what you're supposed to do, but don't become bitter.

Don't think a building is essential for a ministry. You'd be surprised what you can do without one. After walking across America in 1970, I was fasting and praying in Washington together with my wife, Sherry There was a pay telephone right at the corner of Fifteen and Constitution where we were praying. News got out that anyone who had a need could call that pay phone. The Associated Press shot that phone number out all over America on the wire service, and people started to call. Here we were on a little spot of grass along the public sidewalk with the cross leaned up against a tree, fasting and praying. The phone would start ringing and I'd pick it up. "I read in the paper that if anybody needed help, you could help. Well, I don't have any diapers for my baby. Could I have two dozen diapers?" I'd say, "Where are you living? What's your address?" We'd take that down. I'd no sooner put down the phone from that call when the phone would ring again. "Listen, I read in the paper that you're giving stuff away, if anybody needs it. What can I do to help?" "Well, at such and such an address, there's somebody who needs two dozen diapers. Can you take them two dozen diapers? Call back tomorrow, and we'll let you know if anything else is needed." Do you know, we were *inundated.* We were so busy that I had to develop a staff to answer the telephone. So many people were coming to our corner that we had to have workers for three eight-hour shifts per day. That was the only way Sherry and I could get some sleep on the sidewalk. People were coming at all hours of the day and night wanting help, wanting to talk. We did this with no building, just the public phone. We named the place "Jesus Corner," and before long the word was out. "That's Jesus Corner. You can get all kinds of help there at Jesus Corner." All it takes is a burden to reach out and the willingness to pay the price.

You'll Need All the Help You Can Get

You need all the help and support you can get for an outreach ministry. I remember when we started on the Strip, we didn't have any idea how we would get all the food. Sherry and I couldn't afford it. Finally, we thought about all the leftover foods at bakeries so we started to go to them regularly. We'd ask for their leftover food, making it clear that we were giving it away and not selling it. They always gave us food. In fact, we got almost all our food from Jewish bakeries and catering services. One of the managers gave his life to Jesus, his Messiah, and now he's out on the streets witnessing himself. Many of these bakery owners showed a sensitivity to human need. You'll find a lot of people who aren't Christians but who will help you meet human needs. Sometimes they are much more kind and considerate and helpful than a lot of Christians who get off on a spiritual ego trip and look down on everybody else. Quite often they won't reach out and help a needy person. Just because a person hasn't received Christ, that doesn't mean he doesn't have attributes that are beautiful. Just imagine what these people will be like when they know Jesus Christ. If you think they're wonderful now, think how much greater their effectiveness will be when they know Christ, because no matter how good a person is, he isn't all he can be until he is a Christian. That goodness won't be able to take him to heaven anyway. He has to come through repentance and faith in the Lord Jesus.

Be Careful About Financing

You'll have to face the question of financing. I have very strong feelings about this. I just can't stand those Christian ministries that employ an advertising agency. They come up with a slick financing program with computerized mailouts that beg for donations, donations, donations. Once I saw an appeal on television about hunger. I was concerned because I had just been in Africa, so I sent in a check. We talked it over as a family and we came up with a big figure. We were going to do it regularly every Christmas. But do you know what happened? We started getting a thick envelope full of multicolored brochures every month. I wrote about eight months later and said, "Don't send me any more of these. You're spending all I gave you on brochures encouraging me to give. Save the stamps, save the brochures. You're burning me out." But they just kept coming. I knew the guy who ran the ministry, and I wrote him a personal letter and I said, "You can count me out, my dear brother. You're spending all my money on advertising, when I want it to go to those hungry people."

We're living at a time when you can buy mailing lists. There are agencies that exist just to sell the mailing lists of one Christian group to other groups. You can buy those mailing lists and send out half a million letters to Christians who have donated to other ministries. The agency that sells them to you will be able to predict what percentage of them will respond and how much money you'll get back. If the brochure is in black and white, you'll get back so much. If it's in color, you'll get back so much. They've got it down pat. You may put a little picture of Arthur Blessitt on the front with his cross and a bunch of hungry folks. "Help Arthur Blessitt save the world." It'll raise lots of money.

But, I'll tell you, I can't live with it. I can't live with firing out a newsletter and financial appeal to every businessman I meet begging him for a donation. Before long you begin to see people in terms of dollars. You can build a big organization that way. You can put every big-name person you meet on the advisory board, not that they ever advise you. You don't want their advice, you want their money and their influence. When you get ready to raise funds, you call the people who are on your board of advisors, and you put pressure on them and they'll help you raise lots of money.

Of course, it's hard to imagine Jesus doing it that way. So I urge you to try to minister as much as you can, as Jesus would. This is especially important if yours is an evangelistic ministry, because if you don't watch it, you'll become alienated from the churches. If you go into a church and receive an offering and then put all the names and addresses of the church members on your mailing list and start sending them dunning letters, before long no church will let you in. You'll be raking off the church's finances and hurting their ministry. I advise you not to worry a lot about money. Just be faithful to what God's leading you to do, and God will take care of you. Don't get into begging, because that doesn't show faith in God. Minister the work of Christ as He leads you, and do it wisely and effectively. Then, God will meet your needs. There may be temporary problems, but in the long run you'll never have to say, "My Father has denied me my needs." You'll say, "Wow, why has God been so good to me? I don't deserve it." You won't have to start scheming and conning and tricking to get money. Just be straightforward in your ministry.

Push Your People Out of the Building

One of the pitfalls you'll have to watch out for is the tendency of the Christians to want to stay in their nice, comfortable fellowship. Your ministry can turn into a praise group that's worthless for outreach. Now it's all right to have a prayer and praise fellowship sometimes, but if that's *all* you do, you might as well shut down. Don't let your witness ministry just become a big hallelujah group that never gets out the door. If you're not careful, you'll lose sight of your original purpose.

In Northern Ireland, we had a lot of converts from both the Catholic and the Protestant side. For the first time, some of these people were enjoying fellowship across denominational lines. They were really into this new relationship.

But we made a rule right at the beginning. We said that, at least for the first few weeks after conversion, no one should spend more than an hour in a prayer or Bible study group. I didn't want them meeting and praying and having big Bible studies and never getting out in the streets to do witnessing. Do you know, this has exploded and exploded. Some of the groups have run up to a hundred and then they have divided into smaller groups. There's tremendous unity that comes from the community reaching out for Jesus Christ together. Now it is common to see continual witnessing by groups and individuals in all areas of Northern

Ireland, on both sides, Catholic and Protestant. Protestants witness on the Catholic side and Catholics on the Protestant side. They're all out together because they started as an outreach ministry and that's what they remained.

3

WITNESSING EFFECTIVELY

8
Materials You'll Need

The Message Is More Important Than the Method

There is nothing that is essential for bringing someone to Christ except the conveying of the knowledge of Christ to them in whatever manner you can. That's why we call witnessing "sharing Jesus Christ." You don't have to have a gospel tract in order to lead a person to Jesus. You don't have to have a Jesus sticker to be a witness. You don't even have to have the Bible in your hand. All you really need is Jesus in your heart. You must keep reminding yourself that it's not the technique or the material that leads a person to Christ. It is the witness of another person who already knows Jesus.

There have been times when I've witnessed to people and it was so dark I couldn't even read the Bible in my hand. Still, they've been saved. There have been times I've led people to Jesus Christ even though I didn't have a Bible with me. There have been other times when I have just talked and shared Christ and never opened my Bible even though I held it in my hand. There is no fixed approach, no accepted system that will bring people to Jesus Christ. Many times Christians become locked into one means of communication and begin to think that that technique itself is the only right way to witness. But I believe two persons can have totally different approaches in sharing Christ and be equally effective. So you don't have to witness like Arthur Blessitt in order to be a witness for Jesus Christ and to win people to Him. You don't have to witness like Billy

Graham or Bill Bright or like any other evangelist who is effective. You allow God to use *you* for His glory and let the witness of Christ be translated through your personality as you share Christ.

And yet, there are a number of materials that can make your witnessing much more effective. Some of these can go places that you can't. They can stay after you leave. The ones we'll be discussing here have been successfully used in many different situations. I think they will assist you in your witnessing.

Don't Go to Battle Without Your Sword

The Bible is the single most important material we need when we are witnessing. As a matter of fact, I *always* carry the Bible with me. I have both a big Bible and a small pocket Bible which is just a New Testament. Many times when I'm on the road walking, carrying the cross, I can't take the big Bible because there's no room for it. I just carry the small one covered with a plastic case. The plastic cover is a precaution against rain. I can get soaking wet and my Bible will still be usable. Some people say the print is so small that they can't read it. Well, I holler loud enough so they can hear it even if they can't read it.

When I'm witnessing on the streets or in homes, I usually carry the big Bible. I'm especially careful to do this in areas where I think there might be trouble. I don't want people to misunderstand who I am or what I'm doing there. They all know what a Bible is, and it reassures them that you aren't a threat to them.

Maybe some of you will never go into areas like this, but if you're going after street people you're bound to be in some difficult situations. You may be with a bunch of people who are involved with drugs. They're always looking around for narcotics agents, so they're suspicious of you. If you keep your Bible in your pocket and just mumble a few phrases like, "Have you ever thought of spiritual things?" you're liable to end up with someone pounding you on the head. They'll think you're a narcotics agent. But if you carry your Bible right up front, you can avoid that kind of problem.

When I go into go-go clubs and places like that, I hold the Bible so that they can see it. Then when I'm talking to the girls, they're never under any illusion as to what my purpose is. If you keep your Bible in your hand while you're witnessing, it'll defeat the devil. It will put people under conviction, and they won't be able to change the subject. It's dangerous to try to witness in such places without identifying yourself right up front. Some people go into a bar or nightclub without carrying a Bible or having some Jesus stickers or other Christian symbol. They just sit at the bar and drink cokes, trying to get to know people, to become their friends. They're just waiting for an opportunity for witness to open up. But it's very easy to get caught up in the spirit of the place. If you go into the devil's den and start visiting and socializing, you're likely to wind up just like the people you are witnessing to. I've seen it happen over and over again.

To prevent this, always go in with your Bible in your hand. As soon as you sit down, start witnessing to the person nearest to you — right away! Then, there will be no question to you or to them about what you're there for. You're there to win souls. And as soon as you finish witnessing, leave.

On the street, the Bible can have another very practical use. If you are involved in a confrontation with someone, and he's coming after you, just put the Bible up in front of your face and say, "God bless you, praise the Lord." They don't know what you're doing, but you've got the Bible up there sort of to protect you. They'll have to hit the Word if they want to hit you. They won't do it. You can just calmly back away. Sometimes I've been out on the streets and a hooker has tried to get a hold of me. I say, "Hey, look, if you want to hold on to something, hold on to the Bible!" It bugs them to death. So, keep the Word in your hand.

Even when I'm traveling, I carry my Bible and cover my bags with Jesus stickers. Then, when I find my seat on the airplane, the person sitting next to me sees the Bible and the stickers and starts squirming. He knows I'm there for Jesus. In this way, I avoid all kinds of temptations, simply because people know I'm a Christian right from the beginning. I've found that the more conspicuous I am, the more effective I am.

Those Little Paper Evangelists

Gospel tracts can strengthen your personal witness. Sometimes people who will not listen to you will read them. It doesn't matter who wrote them or how fancy they are, as long as they clearly point out the way of salvation.

I recommend using tracts that are inexpensive. That way you can be a good steward of your money, and you will have more to spend on buying Bibles, which are the *best* gospel tracts. Commercial tracts cost five or ten cents apiece, and at that rate you can easily spend a few dollars a day. But if you use an inexpensive tract, you can give out far more for less money.

The best solution to this problem is to have your own tracts printed. Design one yourself and have a local printer typeset and produce it. The greater the volume you print, the lower the price. So, you're better off saving your money and buying 10,000 or 20,000 than just having a few hundred done.

What should be included in an ideal tract? First and most essential, there must be a clear outline of how a person can receive Christ. This is very important when you give a tract to someone who won't listen to you talk. When he goes to his house or motel and reads it, he will know how to be saved. A gospel tract should present the way of salvation so clearly that a person can understand step one, step two, step three, step four, how to be saved.

Secondly, there should be a prayer that a person can use in accepting Christ. Most people don't have any idea how to pray. They don't know that prayer is just a simple conversation with God. The prayer in your gospel tract will put words in their mouth so that they can pray for salvation.

I was seven years old when I accepted Christ. An evangelist talked to me in the church parking lot and led me to Jesus. I had wanted to receive Him, but I didn't know what to say to God in prayer. The evangelist gave me the words and I prayed them. You'll probably never know how many people use the simple prayer in your tract to receive Christ.

Thirdly, every gospel tract should have some simple statement on follow-up — what a person should do now that he has accepted Christ. You've got to help a new convert get started. He may not have any local fellowship to help him.

Finally, you should always include a return address or telephone number. It may be your church or your outreach center or your own home. But, it's important that an interested person know how to get more help if he needs it.

The Big Question

The tract we have developed and have used by the thousands is entitled "The Big Question." The front attracts a person's attention with a large question mark. He wonders what the big question is, so he opens the tract.

Here is the question that confronts him:

> If you had died the minute you started to read this, do you have the assurance that you would be in heaven?

Of course, if he is not a Christian, he has no assurance about eternity. So, he wants to know how he can have some assurance.

Without beating around the bush, the tract immediately tells him. The answer begins with the words, "The Bible says," so that the person will know he is not just reading the opinions of men. Four Bible verses tell him the steps to salvation: (1) All have sinned (Romans 3:23); (2) The wages of sin is death (Romans 6:23); (3) God showed that He loves us by sending Christ to die for our sins (Romans 5:8); (4) Any one who calls upon Him will be saved from his sin (Romans 10:13).

Then the tract invites the person to simply trust Christ. And, a prayer of acceptance is given:

> Dear Jesus, forgive me all my sins and save my soul. I repent of all my sins and ask you to come into my heart and be the Lord of my life. Take control of my life, for I give myself to Thee. Thank you for hearing my prayer and saving my soul. In Jesus' name I pray. Amen.

If he has accepted Christ, he is asked to fill in his name and address and mail it in to the address on the back.

Finally, there is a brief follow-up guide. It encourages the new convert to: (1) Pray daily; (2) Read the Bible daily; (3) Witness for Christ daily; (4) Attend a church where the Bible is preached and Christ is honored; (5) Keep Christ's commandments.

The New Life

Because there is quite often no local fellowship for a new convert to relate to, we have also developed a more detailed follow-up tract, entitled "The New Life." When we lead a person to Christ on the street, we want him to have as much help as possible getting started in the Christian life.

This follow-up tract has three sections. The first reviews what has happened when he accepted Christ and helps him, through selected Scripture verses,* to become assured of his salvation. The second section encourages him to be filled with the Holy Spirit as he lives his new life (Ephesians

*For Scripture references, see page 205.

5:18). The third is a more detailed explanation of the follow-up steps listed in the other tract.

> On the back of the tract is my name and address and a personal greeting: "I challenge you to let Jesus fill your life and to seek to walk in His will. The coming of the Lord draweth near. May we bear effective witness of Him until that moment when we shall stand in His presence in Heaven. It is a joy to have you as a new brother or sister in Christ Jesus. May the grace of the Lord Jesus Christ and the power of the Holy Spirit fill you and strengthen you in Jesus' Name.
>
> Arthur Blessitt.
> Luke 18:1

I don't believe this tract takes the place of good personal follow-up, but it will help a person who would otherwise be floundering all by himself. A convert needs to know right away that Jesus is with him, that God's Spirit is in him, so that he doesn't feel all alone. He needs to know that his sins are forgiven. He needs to know that God has saved him and that he's received eternal life. He needs to know that he's a child of God, that he's in the family of God. He needs to know how to be filled with the Spirit and to walk in the Spirit. He needs to know what to do to develop that kind of a life.

If possible, I also like to give a new convert a Bible — at least a New Testament. You're encouraging him to read the Bible, but he may not have one. This is difficult when you're working out on the street, but you may be able to keep them in your car nearby. When you give him a Bible, you should share a brief little explanation of what the Bible is and why it is so important. Otherwise, he may open it up to some genealogies and become discouraged. Then, he'll flip over to Revelation and see monsters that scare and confuse him. You need to guide him where to read first.

What in the World Are "Jesus Stickers?"

I guess I'm the world's number one user of Jesus stickers. They're little pieces of paper with glue on the back that have a simple attention-getting message: JESUS LOVES YOU; TURN ON TO JESUS; SMILE—GOD LOVES YOU.

I began the first Jesus sticker movement. The Lord burdened my heart back in the mid 60's to start printing something for Christians to wear, because everybody else was wearing badges of various kinds, with dirty slogans, profane words and things like that. It was during the hippie era. I thought up an inexpensive way to advertise Jesus. I was in the supermarket one day, and I saw little price tags stuck on all the cans, and I thought, "Those would really work with a gospel slogan on them. I wonder how much they cost." I couldn't afford any kind of pin at that time. So we experimented and printed some Jesus stickers. I've changed a few of the symbols along the way, but I've found that these stickers are one of the most effective means of making contact with people for the gospel.

One night the police on Hollywood Boulevard said to me, "Listen, what in the world is happening? Every pimp, every hooker in the streets is wearing Jesus stickers. Do you just give them to the bad sinners or to everybody?" It's really strange, but the worst sinners will take the stickers more quickly than anybody. It is easier to give them out to drunks than it is to church members walking the sidewalk. Christians are a little leery. They say, "Now what's written on that?" The drunks say, "Put them all over me." They'll stick them on the seat of their pants — all over. But, I don't mind. The slogans can speak for themselves no matter who's wearing them.

Of course, just because a guy wears a sticker on the seat of his pants that doesn't mean he's saved.

I meet people all the time who have stickers on their refrigerators or on their bed or on their dresser mirror or on their car dash. Some people put them everywhere, and yet they haven't been saved even though those stickers have been there for years. It takes more than a sticker to lead a person to Christ. The sticker just opens the door.

That's why I have my own stickers printed with my name and address on each one. Many people have written me letters for more information. When I was in Australia, there was a whole group of churches that wanted Jesus stickers. I gave them a few, but I encouraged them to print their own with their address on them. People don't have to write to America. We did the same thing in England. We gave away over a million stickers there, but I refused to let them put my address on them. They did their own. Otherwise, I would have been inundated. As it is, we get mail from all around England, all over Europe, all over the world as a result of Jesus stickers.

The main reason for giving out stickers when you're witnessing is to get a person to stop so you can talk to him. If you're on a busy street, with people rushing by, you need to hand a person something interesting to get him to slow down for a minute. If you don't have a sticker or tract just say, "Will you stop and let me talk with you for a minute?" He won't know what you're up to. Maybe you're trying to pick him up or make a drug contact.

But, the sticker overcomes that problem. The person can see right away that you're not doing anything threatening. You may say, "I'd like to give you a sticker." They'll look at it—"What is this, anyway?" And then you start to witness, "It says, *JESUS LOVES YOU*. Do you know Him in your heart?"

And the stickers also multiply your witness. They make people on the street notice that there are a group of Christians down there witnessing.

People come walking down the street with stickers on. One, two, three, four—one person after another has a red badge on. "What's going on here? Where'd you get that?" "Oh, a guy down the street stuck it on me." And it won't be three hours before the whole town knows you're there. People will be wearing stickers all around town. And others will ask, "Where'd you get that?" "Well, there's a guy down there at the corner telling people about Jesus." The whole town will be aware that you're there witnessing without your ever leaving that corner. If you do it on a regular basis, say, every Saturday, they'll expect you to be there each week. As soon as they see the stickers, they'll say, "Uh, oh, I know they're still down there. Here comes another sticker." You'll get people thinking about Jesus who had never thought about Him before.

Does Music Help?

I'm discussing music among materials for witnessing because it can be used as an aid for spreading the good news about Jesus, just as tracts and stickers can. However, it can be as much of a liability as an asset in street ministry. If you're going to have a musical program and witness afterwards, that's great. But a guy who's walking the street with a guitar strung over his shoulder has a hard time sticking to witnessing. Before long he's back to strumming the guitar again, singing instead of witnessing.

But at the beach a guitar can be a big help. A few Christians can sit down and do a little singing, and a group will gather around. Then one of the Christians can tell them how to know Jesus Christ, and a lot of one-on-one witnessing can grow from this spontaneous meeting.

Singing can be effective on the street and in clubs and bars, but I like to do it without a guitar. If you have a guitar, the people expect you to be good. We've had about ten people all singing off key, and yet we've sung in places where no trained choir could get to sing. We just start singing, and some drunks will say, "Do you know 'The Old Rugged Cross?' " So we sing it. Sometimes a crowd gathers and I have a chance to preach.

The most effective use of music in witnessing is spontaneous and from your heart. Just enjoy the Lord, and if you feel like singing, sing. This kind of music is not a technique, but a natural expression of your joy in Christ.

9

Leading a Person to Christ

Make Sure You Have Only One Purpose

Leading a person to Christ is *leading* a person to Christ. It is not teaching him about the latest Christian fad. It is not telling him all the ways in which you think his life needs to change. You need to discipline yourself to focus on your one purpose—you want to lead him to Christ.

There are plenty of tangent issues you can get into. There is no group in the world that gets off on more wild horses than Christian groups. Go down to the Christian book store and see what most of the materials are about. At one time, tongues are in; a little later healing is in; the next year body life is in; then Christian fellowship; then baptism; then the Second Coming is the big thing. If you just watch, you'll see that Christians are always running from one fad to another. Christians will just confuse you with all these side issues and their "in" subject of the year. You'll just be riding one wave after another.

Added to these Christian fads, you will have more pressure coming from whatever is the "in thing" on the streets. For a while, massage parlors were all the rage. Some Christians wanted to crusade against them, but if you build your ministry around a cause like that, it will soon be irrelevant. Massage parlors are no longer in. Other fads, like nude night clubs and psychedelic shops, have come and gone. If you make sure your ministry is directed toward helping lead people to Christ, you'll be effective year after year, having results for God, whatever the current issues are.

Right now, a lot of Christians are busy fighting homosexuals. We're not called to fight gays, we're called to win the world to Jesus Christ. It doesn't matter what a person's hang-up is. The guy driving a new car who's hung up on money is just as needy as a homosexual. Even little children who are not saved are in the same shape. Our attitude toward the community is to win individuals to Jesus Christ. I could be out fighting all the gays on Hollywood Boulevard. As it is, we're down there witnessing to them every night. And they are listening. If I'm talking with a guy and he says, "But, I'm gay," I respond, "Praise the Lord, I'm happy too!" And then we get back to the subject of how he can receive Jesus Christ. We're not called to preach Anita Bryant; we're called to preach Jesus.

Some people just want to talk. They'll get you into politics or sports or different religions, and before you know it your conversation is roving all over the world and you never get to Jesus Christ. If you're not careful, the devil will have you yak, yak, yakking about every other subject under the sun.

So, learn to stick with what God has called you to do—to lead people to Christ. After they've received Him, He will open their eyes and begin to rebuild their lives. Then they can start dealing with the various problem areas in their lives.

When I go out to witness I intend to lead to Christ every person I witness to. That is my objective. My goal is not to lead to Christ *half* of those with whom I share Christ, or one out of every ten. I pray and plan to win *every person* I talk to. I want them all to be saved. I believe that's the scriptural viewpoint. God is not willing that any should perish (2 Peter 3:9), so I shouldn't be willing that any perish. You may know in your mind that not all will respond, but in your heart, you are anxious to win everyone. So, at the beginning of every conversation, you should visualize the person praying to receive Christ at the end.

The Time to Witness Is Now!

You don't know whether the person you're talking to will be alive or dead tomorrow. So, unless he stops you, lead right through to the point of receiving Jesus.

Some people have a casual attitude about witnessing. "I'm going to sow a little seed and share a little word about Jesus. Then, maybe someone else will sow a little more seed, and another person a little more. Someday one of those seeds will grow and the person will be saved." The purpose of a Christian doing this kind of witnessing is not to lead people to Jesus, but to kind of sow a little seed and put a little word out. Well, I beliive you can sow a little seed, and God can water it and it can spring up and bear fruit *within three minutes*, or in even a shorter time. It doesn't take days, weeks or years. A person can be saved in one conversation, and that should be our objective. Maybe they won't respond as we know they can and should. Then we should keep the door open so that we can come back again and try to win them then. But, at the beginning, our purpose should be to go all the way through with them, that they might be saved.

The importance of pressing for decisions *now* grows as we remind ourselves that everyone needs to be saved. The Bible convinces us that people without Jesus are lost. "The wages of sin is death" (Romans 6:23); "The soul that sinneth, it shall surely die " (Ezekiel 18:20). And just as clearly as the Bible teaches that every person without Christ is lost, it also teaches that any individual can be saved right now: "Behold, now is the day of salvation, now is the accepted time" (2 Corinthians 6:2). So, I assume it is God's will for me to witness to every person I meet unless God specifically tells me not to.

Many Christians wake up in the morning with no intention of sharing Jesus Christ with someone during that day. They're going to wait for a tingling of the spirit in their backbone, or some super emotional experience that turns them on. Otherwise, they won't tell anybody about Jesus. There's no indication in the Bible that the only time you are to witness is when you feel some tingling or a special feeling or have a vision or see fire dancing over someone's head that tells you, "That's the one!" Now, God does lead us by His Holy Spirit, but He doesn't want us to sit around passively until He zaps us. The normal policy of a believer's life should be to share Jesus Christ with everyone he meets during the day until God's Spirit clearly tells him not to. Everyone is a prospect for salvation.

Speak to a Person's Heart, Not to His Appearance

If you're not careful, you will treat people differently just based on their appearance. Train yourself to speak to their hearts, not to what you see on the surface. You meet a big guy, about 6'7" tall and 290 lbs., muscles bulging out, and a big full beard. Your natural response may be, "Wow, that guy is tough and mean." So, you may not try to witness to him. And yet under that big body may be a person who's scared of life and hungry for salvation. Inside, he may be just a big baby, but you've been intimidated by his physical appearance. Or, you may be talking to a girl who you figure will just be the next Miss America. She's a knockout. And yet in her heart she may not have any beauty at all. She may feel dirty and sinful and ashamed.

Don't let people's outside appearance intimidate you—their build, their skin color, their style of clothes, their language. Speak to their hearts. They may try to put you off with conversation, saying they're not interested in religion at all. Yet, the person inside may be crying out for you to keep talking about Jesus. They may be talking from the head about all sorts of things, but you just keep talking to their hearts about the love of God. They may run down churches, preachers, Christians. Just ignore their words and keep talking to their hearts.

I met a guy on the beach once who was giving me a hard

time. He said, "I'd like to get some little green devil badges and follow you around. I'd put one over every one of your Jesus stickers." He wasn't smiling, he was serious. I said, "Really?" He said, "Yeah, you must have a millionaire financing you to put all these out." I said, "More than a millionaire. God's financing me; you know, the One who runs this world. Maybe you can get the devil to finance your green ones."

I could see he was interested, or he wouldn't still be talking to me, so I said, "Listen, I'd love to have you follow along behind me with your green stickers. You're liable to be saved. I've never seen the devil follow a Christian long, because he's scared." And, I started talking to his heart, sharing Jesus with him. He was really open and we talked for a long time and parted as friends.

One time on Sunset Strip I met a girl outside of a club and started to witness to her. She was dressed and made up in a way that indicated she really thought she was something. She tried to act as if she wasn't interested in what I was saying, but I could tell she was, so I kept talking to her heart. All of a sudden, her boyfriend returned from parking the car and tried to take her into the nightclub. She said, "Wait a minute. I'm talking to this guy."

When he left, she told me, "I was in a convent for three years. It was the happiest time of my life. I used to sing about Jesus, I used to study about Him. It was just wonderful." Tears welled up in her eyes. She said, "I wish I could live it now that I'm out of the convent. I wish I had that now." She had been talking up on one level—chat, chat, chat, chat, chat. But, I was down on another level, talking to her heart. All that sophistication was a cover-up, because she'd been with people who knew Jesus, and she knew that was real life. Finally, we had a prayer together and she felt wonderful. She said she was going to go back and talk to some of her old friends in the convent so that she could continue her Christian growth.

I found that many of the dancers in night clubs grew up

in fundamentalist Christian homes. In their hearts, they feel that they've stumbled and they're unworthy. They feel totally rotten. They try to come across as very hard, but they're not. Many times the people who appear to be the hardest are really the most sensitive.

Henry was one of those tough looking guys. He was in our center on Sunset Strip one night and he really tore into another guy. We had to call an ambulance for him. Afterwards, I called Henry into my office and said, "Henry, you know how hard it is for us to keep this place going. We can't afford to have trouble in here. Why'd you hit him in this place where we're trying to work for the Lord?"

Do you know what happened? This tough, mean-looking guy couldn't even talk. He became all choked up and started to cry. He said, "He was making fun of my girlfriend who's in jail." He cried like a baby, because that's what Henry was inside—a big baby. He had grown up on the streets without a mother or father. He was a terribly lonely person. Then he met a girl who had been kind to him and loved him. Now she was in jail—the only person in the whole world who had ever cared for him. A guy made fun of her, and whammo! Inside the tough hard Henry was a lonely, hurting Henry. I talked to that inner Henry, and he gave his life to Jesus. Since then, he's been witnessing all over.

Don't Wait for the Ideal Situation

The best circumstance for witnessing is when you're one-on-one with another person and neither of you is distracted by anything. I would consider the ideal situation to be sitting down in someone's living room, where he's comfortable. He has called me and invited me to come to his house and explain to him how to be saved. The television is off, and the children are asleep. There is nothing to distract you from quietly opening the Bible together. Once in a while you'll get that kind of an opportunity, but not often.

Most of your witnessing will be under one kind of pressure or another. That's the way life is. You may give a tract to the driver of a bus you're on. You ask, "Do you know Jesus in your heart?" "No, I don't, I really don't." "Well, you can open your heart to Jesus Christ and be saved right now." By this time, you may be getting off the bus. You've got an airplane to catch, and he's got to continue on his route. Cars are piled up behind him. You don't have the time to go from Genesis to Revelation. You don't have the time to do anything but pray right now. You either have to do it quickly or not do it at all. So, you say, "I'd love to pray with you right now," and the guy agrees. Tears are streaming down his cheeks. You grab his hand, and lead him in the sinner's prayer. You give him a gospel tract and a follow-up tract and say, "My address is on the back." The guy's revving up the motor. He's got to go. Cars are honking. "God bless you, brother," and you step off.

Often in Hollywood we see a big limousine pull up to pick up people from a nightclub. I greet the people as they're getting in and stick a tract in the window. Maybe one girl in the back seat will show an interest in receiving Jesus. The driver is saying, "Come on, let's get out of here. We don't need to listen to a blankety-blank preacher." The girl says, "That's *exactly* what I need." So, as the driver is trying to pull away, I pray with her as fast as I can. Believe it or not, God saves people under circumstances like that.

Sometimes in clubs the music is so loud you have to shout to be heard. The people are jammed in body to body. You give out tracts and stickers until someone seems to show a little interest. Then you cup your hands to his ear and ask, "Are you saved?" These aren't ideal conditions for witnessing, but you still try your best.

Sometimes you're talking with someone who's so drunk he can't stand up. You're talking to him, and the guy's drunk, and his hearing aid's out of his ear, and his glasses are on crooked.. Most Christians would walk by him. He's too drunk, no hope for that old guy. Let me tell you, when he buys a cup of coffee for twenty cents and he gets back twenty cents change from a half dollar, he'll put up a squawk. Who are you to determine that he can't be saved? Nothing's lost if you pray with him and he doesn't understand you.

I've prayed with people others thought were dead. I knelt down and whispered a prayer in their ear, and invited them to trust Christ. If they're not conscious, nothing's lost, and if they are, it's worth the effort. Sometimes when a guy is dead drunk, totally incoherent, I stick tracts in all his pockets. Then I wheel off a bunch of Jesus stickers and stick them all over him. When he sobers up the next day he'll think he's been to church.

You've heard of a pickpocket. Well, I'm a "putpocket." I can stand and talk to a guy who doesn't want a tract, and I'll guarantee that I'll get five on him before he knows. A guy will say, "Listen, I don't want one of those stickers." I pat him on the back and say, "God bless you, brother," and he's going on down the street with one on his back. I'll have one in my hand and shake hands with a guy, and he'll have a sticker on his hand. Then, when he's looking at his hand, I'll put one somewhere else. A putpocket for the Lord.

Deal with Distractions

Even though you shouldn't wait for the ideal kind of situation to witness, quite often you can improve the atmosphere for witnessing by a little creative thought. For instance, if two of you are witnessing to a little group of people, and one seems very interested, but the others are arguing and causing a problem, one of you can draw the arguers away so the other can lead the interested person to Christ. You can just throw out a question to get them talking to you so your friend can be free to deal with the sincere seeker.

Maybe two of you are witnessing to a lady in her home. She's interested, but the baby is fussing and that distracts her. One of you can pick up the baby and cuddle it. You may even learn how to change diapers to see someone's soul saved. Just work on it until you figure it out, while the lady is listening to the message of Jesus Christ.

If a guy's stuck by the road with a flat tire, don't just preach at him while he's sweating to fix it. Get down there and work with him—in fact work harder than he does. Then he'll be more likely to listen as you share.

When you visit someone in the hospital with broken bones from an accident, don't talk about his physical problems: "How're you doing today? Oh, you look a mess, don't you? Tell me what happened." They don't need that. With the joy of the Lord, just visit them a minute and then start sharing about Jesus Christ. You don't have to rehash everything that's happened. All their friends have already been in and asked them what happened to their leg and their arm. They're tired of telling the story. They want a little good news. Concentrating on their physical problems distracts them from their deeper spiritual need.

There Is No Magic Plan

There is no one plan or program for leading a person to Jesus Christ. A lot of people have been through a training session and have learned a way to share Jesus. Then they conclude that's the only right way. Now, every method that works is good. There's no bad way to lead someone to Christ. If you're using an approach that shares how to receive Jesus and it's working for you, then Praise the Lord. But don't think yours is the only way. You may be a four-step person. Don't try to persuade others that four steps are better than seven steps. These methods are just man's way of trying to share God's truths.

I am going to share with you the method we have developed, but I want to make it clear that this is *a* way to witness, not *the* way. The outline in our method is just there as a simple guideline so that you can take an interested person through to the place where he is sure he's saved.

After you use this a while, you may want to expand on it or discard it completely and just use your Bible.

The Big Question

Our introductory tract, "The Big Question," has been described in chapter 8. Now I want to tell you how you can use it.

When I give one of these to a person, I don't use the word "tracts," because most people don't know what that means. I say, "I'd like to give you this handbill." I've found it even simpler just to say, "I'd like to give you this." "This" calls his attention to the piece of paper you've put in his hand, and he's almost forced to look at it.

Sometimes a person will ask what the big question is, and sometimes he'll open it and find out for himself. But quite often you'll have to take the initiative. "Do you know what the big question is?" Then, tell him.

> If you had died the minute you started to read this, do you have the assurance that you would be in heaven?

The reason we start off with this particular question is that it immediately gets away from questions about denominationalism or church affiliation. You're not dealing with whether the person is Protestant or Catholic; you're not dealing with the person as Protestant or Catholic; you're not dealing with his church situation, but with his relationship with God. If you start by inviting a person to your church or outreach center, you'll get into one big fuss after another. Most people aren't interested in your building. They go to ballgames on Sunday. What have you got that's attractive to them? Only Jesus.

Most people respond to the big question by admitting that they don't know. Some people will say, "I hope so," or, "Well, I want to." Very few will say, "Yes, I know if I died I'd go to heaven." You might get that answer if you were around churches, but in the streets you seldom do.

If the person says, "Yes, I do have the assurance that I'd

go to heaven," then I prod them in a kindly way. "How do you know that you would spend eternity with God if you died right now? What do you base that on?" If the person is a Christian, that will give him an opportunity to give testimony. If he's got something to say, he can say it then. If he's not a Christian, he may say, "Well, I'm as good as anybody around here, and if anyone makes it, I will." Now, *you* know that that's not what's going to qualify him for heaven. It's receiving Christ, and knowing Him. But it's not wise to say, "Hey man, you're a liar." You know from his answer that he needs to understand how to receive Jesus, so you very politely say, "Well, I'd like to show you a scripture verse here. 'For all have sinned and come short of the glory of God.' I'm a sinner, you're a sinner. . . ." And you just go right into the witness as though they'd said they didn't know where they were going after death.

If the person has shown by his testimony that he's saved, that's an ideal time for you to say, "Well, wonderful. Are you active in sharing Jesus Christ?" And many times he will say, "I do know Jesus. I've trusted Him as my Lord. But no, I'm not actively sharing Him." You say, "Well, listen, let me give you a few of these, and you can give some of them out on the street yourself. Take these and tell your friends about Christ." That way you get him started witnessing. You get him involved. If you meet a person who knows Christ, don't have the attitude, "I can't talk to you because there's nothing wrong with you." Let the Lord use you to get him involved. Ask him if he's regularly attending a local fellowship, and if he's not, encourage him into it. And pray with Christians you meet. Sometimes the person has really backslid and meeting you is an important part of his coming back to the Lord.

The Four Salvation Verses

In our tract, "The Big Question," the way of salvation is presented through four simple Bible verses (see chapter 8).

I encourage you to open the tract when you're witnessing and point to the verses one at a time. It's even better if you flip to the verses in your Bible while they're following them in the tract. That makes it clear to them that the verses actually do come from God's Word.

The first thing a person must know in order to go to heaven is found in Romans 3:23: "For all have sinned and fall short of the glory of God." Read the verse, then tell the person, "It says that *all* have sinned. That means that *I'm* a sinner and *you're* a sinner." When you begin this way, you overcome the attitude that just because you're witnessing you think you're more righteous than he is—holy, holy, holy. You're admitting that you're a sinner, and that makes it easier for him to admit that he is, too. Quite often at this time the guy will actually be nodding in agreement.

Sometimes a wise guy will say, "I've never sinned; I'm no sinner." I just tap him on the chest and say, "Hey, man, you're smarter than that. You know better than that." Then I move right on to the second verse without arguing with him. Deep within, every person knows that he's a sinner.

At this point, some people will want to begin talking about their specific sins, saying, "I'm this," or "I'm that." Just say, "Listen, God says He will deal with all our sins," and move on. Don't let them get you off on a tangent, dwelling on their sins.

The second thing a person needs to know is that the wages of sin is death, but God wants to give us eternal life through Christ (Romans 6:23). This shows the seriousness of sin, that it has built a barrier between us and Him. The consequence is death and hell, separation from God.

But the verse also shows that God has done something about the barrier. He has given us a gift of eternal life through Jesus Christ. So, there's a choice here—death or life, sin or Christ.

I move pretty quickly on to the third thing a person needs to know. "But God commended His love toward us, in that while we were yet sinners, Christ died for us"

(Romans 5:8). I tell the person, "God loves us, and He did something about our condition." I explain as much as I can about who Jesus is and why He died.

Then, the fourth verse brings them to the point of decision. "For whosoever shall call upon the name of the Lord shall be saved" (Romans 10:13). Tell him, "You can be saved *now*. You can receive Him as your Savior *this moment*." I don't spend a lot of time talking about it; I just invite them to do it.

A Salvation Diagram

Sometimes I use an even simpler approach, based on only one verse, Romans 6:23. I do this when I am really rushed and don't have much time to get the message across.

I'll grab a piece of paper—maybe a napkin, or the back of a tract—and draw this diagram:

SATAN	*GOD*
SIN	*GIFT*
WAGES	*ETERNAL LIFE*
DEATH	*JESUS CHRIST*
LOST!	*SAVED!*

I talk about it as I'm drawing. "We've all sinned, haven't we? When you sin, you receive wages—death. On the other side is a gift. God has already offered it to you. You haven't earned it; Jesus did. But, you must *receive* Him." At this point, I usually hand the person something to show how he has to receive it.

I continue, "Everyone is by nature on the left side (LOST!). But, we can get across the barrier to the other side (SAVED!). We can't *do* anything to get across—the CROSS of Jesus is right here in the middle." Then I complete the diagram:

SATAN	GOD
SIN	GIFT
WAGES	ETERNAL LIFE
DEATH	JESUS CHRIST
LOST!	SAVED!

Now I zero in. "Right now, which side are you on? You *want* to be over here, don't you? Then why don't you ask Jesus to put you over here right now?" At this point, I press for a decision just as I would using "The Big Question."

Praying for Salvation

I always invite a person to pray for salvation right there on the spot. Some Christians are nervous about praying in bars or places like that. I say you can pray anywhere. At times, the person you're leading to Christ will say, "I can't pray in a bar." I say, "Then let's go outside." And we do. One night a guy said to me, "The Bible says you should just pray in your closet." I took him by the arm and said, "Let's go find a closet." The guy said, "No, no, that's not what I meant." He was just trying to get out of making the decision.

Sometimes a person will say, "I'm not worth praying for. I'm just too bad." I respond, "Don't say that. God loves you. If He wants to live in you, you must be good enough. He said, 'Whosoever.' "

People need a little prodding at the point of decision. Don't give them a whole lot of time to consider ways out. Just say, "I'd like to pray for you right now, and I'm sure you don't mind. I want to pray for you first, and then I'll lead you in a simple prayer to help you accept Jesus." Don't ever stop at that point and say, "Would you rather wait or would you like to do it now?" That just is giving the devil an opening at the last minute. Just go ahead and pray. You know that in his heart he wants to receive the Lord, so you pray with him right there.

I like to take the person's hand while I'm praying. Holding his hand doesn't make him any more saved, but it does communicate *love.* That's why I was arrested years ago in Jackson, Mississippi, for shaking a black man's hand. It communicated too much love. I didn't realize a handshake was that powerful, but it is. The sheriff told me I couldn't do that anymore, but I said, "I'm going to shake hands with everybody unless you cut it off. And then I'll stick my nub out. I love people." So, it's a natural thing for me to hold a person's hand while I'm praying for him.

Now, if you feel it's going to cause a problem, don't do it. If you're witnessing to a girl, and the boyfriend's standing over there, prancing around and pouting because he thinks you're liable to get his girlfriend saved and upset everything, you may decide it's wisest not to take her hand. He might think, "I knew it, that guy's just trying to pick her up." Don't get into circumstances if you feel that your actions might be misinterpreted.

When you pray, pray for *them.* Don't pray about your own problems, the church's problems, the world's problems. Sometimes I've been witnessing along with another person, and I want to encourage him, so I ask him to lead in prayer. And he starts in, "Oh, Lord, I'm such a mess. Our church is about to fall apart, God. Revive our people . . ." And, in my heart, I'm praying, "Lord, get him to shut up." Here is a person who wants to get in, and my friend is telling him how bad things are inside. Just pray for that person's salvation; that the power of Satan will be broken in his life, that he'll be free to respond to Jesus.

And, then finish your part of the prayer with, ". . . in Jesus' name." Don't say, "Amen," because then he'll think the prayer is over and start looking around. Without any pause, go on and say, "I'd like to lead you now in this prayer and help you to give your life to Jesus. Now, the prayer is not to me, the prayer is to God. By this prayer, you are inviting the Lord to take over in your heart. I want to help you do that right now." And then pray as though you were him praying, and ask him to repeat the prayer out loud.

This is one good thing about worship in the Catholic Church—they have the people pray out loud. Most Protestant churches don't do this. They believe prayer should be spontaneous. I think that's the ideal, but there are many times when people don't know how to pray or what to pray for. They need to be directed towards specific areas of need.

Some Christians prefer to have a person pray to receive Christ with his own words. I've found that when I do that the person wanders around. He tells the Lord how bad he is, how bad he feels about his old mother he ran away from, and so forth. That's why I've come to use the directed prayer. It gets the person to the point, which is inviting Jesus into his heart.

Emotional Responses Vary

Not everyone has the same emotional reaction after accepting Christ. Some Christians feel that because a person doesn't have tears in his eyes, then God must not be dealing with him. They look for signs and wonders to indicate whether the Lord is working or not. It's not tears that save, it's not a smile that saves, it's the Lord Jesus Christ. You can't tell what's going on in a person's heart just by looking at him.

Many times people do become very emotional at their conversion, and that can be a beautiful thing. I love to talk to somebody and see tears well up in his eyes before we start to pray, then hear him cry while we pray, and then finally see that he's smiling after the prayer. But the night that I trusted the Lord, that didn't happen to me. I didn't cry, I didn't smile, I just prayed and I believed that God was with me. Then I went on home without much emotion.

But He was with me and He still is. Some people may laugh, some people may cry.

Our emotional make-up varies from person to person. Someone may come in right now and say, "Arthur, your wife was just killed," and I would probably start crying. But someone else might react to the news that his wife was killed by immediately working things out in his mind: "Who's taking care of the kids? What funeral director should I call?" Still another person may react by laughing and saying, "Praise the Lord, she's with Jesus." All three of us may love our wives equally, but we have different ways of expressing our emotion.

Review What He's Done

It's good to go over with the new convert what he's done and what has happened to him. After I have prayed with an individual, I look him in the eye and say, "You've received Jesus Christ. Now, God wouldn't lie to you, would He? The Bible says God has forgiven your sin. What's happened to your sin?" "It's forgiven." "And, the Bible says that if you ask Him Jesus will come into your heart. Where is Jesus now?" "He came into my heart." "If you died right now, where would you go?" "Well, I hope it would be heaven." "No, don't hope about it. Jesus is in you, right? Then, if you died, would you take Him to heaven?"

I want to leave a person with the complete assurance that God has heard his prayer and saved his soul.

Get Him Started in the New Life

Then I try to help the person in his first steps in the Christian life. He needs to be told that his new life means following Jesus. I read over with him the suggestions on "The Big Question" tract for beginning a Christian walk (see chapter 8). I encourage him to get into his own prayer and Bible study, be baptized, become part of a local fellowship and live a life of obedience to Jesus' commands.

I think it's a big help to a new convert if you can get him witnessing right away. Sometimes I'll explain to a person that he needs to tell someone about what he's done, then I'll stop the next person who walks by. "Just a minute, brother." The guy will stop and look around, and I'll say, "This friend just did something wonderful. Tell him what you just did." "Well, I just gave my heart to the Lord." Praise the Lord. He's just witnessed. Now, he's broken the ice and the fear is gone. He doesn't have to wait until he's 70, like some people do, before he starts to witness for the first time. If you get him started right, he'll continue doing it.

Sometimes in other countries, I lead a person to the Lord, teach and train him, and send him out to witness. Then, I just pray that he'll never meet any other Christians and learn how red hot he is. He'll think it's normal for a Christian to pray an hour a day, read a few chapters in the Bible, and lead someone to Christ before he goes to bed at night. But if he gets with other Christians, they persuade him he's weird, saying, "You'll mature." That's another way of saying, "You'll soon be dead like me. Then, I'll feel more comfortable around you."

Don't Be Hung Up on Words

No one is saved by using certain words, and no one is lost because he uses other words. A person is either saved or lost because of his heart's response to God. So, a person may have a Christian vocabulary that's different from yours, and yet be just as saved.

As I've traveled around the world, I've met people who have never heard the word "saved," and yet Jesus is their Savior. Others are not familiar with the term "born again." The terminology is not important; it just is one way of expressing the miracle that happens inside a person.

Now, I like the word "saved." I know a lot of people prefer other words, but I like "saved" because it's a biblical word. I like to ask someone, "Are you saved?" Then explain to him how it can happen. But there are people who say the words and have never given their heart to Christ. You've got to get deeper than mere words—to genuine experience.

Don't Argue About the Bible

Sometimes as I begin witnessing by quoting Romans 3:23 from the Bible, the person will say, "Well, I don't believe the Bible." I just ignore it the first time they say it. Then when I read Romans 6:23, they're likely to say again, "I don't believe the Bible." At that point, I will say, "Well, if you don't believe it, then it won't hurt you." And again, I just move ahead with the witness.

If the person is persistent and brings this up the third time, I ask him, "Have you read every word of it?" "No, not every word." "Well, let me read you a little section and see whether it's true or not." I put the Bible right in his lap, and we read the next verse. I ask, "Have you ever read that before?" "No." I'm not arguing with him, but I'm illustrating that he's rejected the Bible without even reading it. In 95% of the cases this kind of approach avoids an argument and allows you to keep witnessing.

Of course if you have to, you can prove that the Bible's the true Word of God. Our faith is based on a solid foundation. But I don't believe very many people have ever been saved by someone sitting down and going through historical documents that prove the Bible is God's Word. When Christ is preached, He draws people to Himself. Then, He'll change their hearts so they accept what the Bible says.

Take Time to Explain Who Jesus Is

A person may be quite ignorant without the Bible and still be saved, but knowledge about Jesus Christ is something else. I believe a person must understand what the Bible teaches about Christ before he can accept Him. If I am witnessing and I feel the person is confused about who Jesus is, I take the time to explain. I tell him that Jesus came in the flesh, was born of the Virgin Mary, lived without sin, died on the cross, rose again and ascended unto the Father. I explain that His Spirit is here now and will dwell in us as we receive Him.

A lady came up to me in England while I was carrying the cross and said, "Can you tell me the end of the story?" I said, "The end of what story?" She said, "I've heard about Jesus being born on Christmas, and I know about Easter when He died, but what ever happened to Him after that?" And, the lady was serious. So, I told her.

On another occasion, I was witnessing to a girl, and we got to the point where I was talking to her about praying and inviting Christ into her heart. She said, "Can I ask a question just before we pray? How can a dead man help me?" I was shocked. She really didn't know that Jesus had risen. I had presumed on her knowledge and she had no idea that He was still around. So, we had to back up and talk about who Jesus is and what He's doing.

Witnessing is sharing *Christ.* If either you or the person you're witnessing to is ignorant about who He is, then you won't really be sharing Him very effectively. So, take the time to make Jesus Christ as clear and understandable as you can. Then, the person will be aware of Who it is he's accepting into his life.

10
Your Personal Life

The first step in any believer's preparation for witness is his own spiritual growth. A new Christian can live off the momentum of his conversion for a few days or a few weeks. He can live on the excitement of having just received Christ, on the knowledge that he's just come into the family of God. But a Christian cannot be an effective witness on a long-term basis without a continuing vitality in his life. A new convert can be as effective as anyone in sharing about his conversion right after he's been saved. He will naturally want to go out and share Jesus. But if he doesn't ever move on from his conversion experience, then he will not mature and develop as he should and he will soon have nothing fresh to share.

The Bible—God's Word to You

It is vital that a person who wants to be a continuing witness become a student of the Word of God. I believe that the Bible is God's word. It is God's message for us. It is the truth. It is infallible in its teaching. It is unerring in its commandments and its direction for our lives. So, in order to be a strong witness for Jesus, a person needs to be a good student of the Word of God. Jesus said, "Man cannot live by bread alone, but by every word that proceedeth from the mouth of God." I cannot emphasize the importance of the Bible enough.

You need to study the Bible in depth. Learn everything you can about it. The best book you can read to learn about the Bible is the Bible itself. There's no book that I or anyone else has written about the Bible that can substitute for reading it directly. I meet a lot of people who read every book going and don't spend much time in the Word. Some of them constantly study cults and doctrines. And they are always running from one Scripture to another without ever studying the Bible systematically, a book at a time. It was written a book at a time and each book contains a specific message because it was written for a particular purpose.

As you study the Bible, focus your attention on the life of Christ. You need to know about Jesus. You should read about Jesus. His life is a well that will never run dry, as you come to understand more and more about Him.

Prayer—Your Words to God

I remember when I was really anxious for the full power of God in my life. I wanted to be the most effective witness possible, a powerful prayer warrior for Jesus. I would meet with some spiritual leader who would lay down and pray. I'd lay down and pray too, but I'd just go to sleep. I'd see others who prayed with their hands up, so I'd raise my hands up, but all I got was tired arms. I'd see others who prayed looking up, and I'd pray looking up, but I got a crick in the neck. Others would pray with their heads bowed. I'd do the same, but I'd go to sleep. I didn't get the power they had.

Then one night in my dorm room at college, I locked the door and experienced an awesome night. I was alone, and I said, "Lord, I'm not leaving this room until I know what it means to be filled with Your Spirit, to walk in Your Spirit, to find that consistent, victorious life." As I was praying, I suddenly clearly understood what a fool I'd been. It seemed as though the Lord said, "You're so hard-headed. If you want to know how to pray, pray like me." And I realized that I had never thought of that. Oh, Jesus was my Lord, but He wasn't my example. So I started studying all the passages about Jesus praying. I analyzed when He prayed, and where He prayed, and how long He prayed. I just decided I was going to pray as Jesus did, and I have had a glorious and marvelous experience since then.

Jesus went off and prayed all night in the mountains, and we also should occasionally go off and pray in the mountains all night. We see Him praying alone. We see Him praying in public. Look at Jesus, then pray as He did.

You need to develop a *life* of prayer, just as Jesus did. This requires discipline. I don't like to waste any time. It took about twenty minutes to drive from my house to where I was working on the Strip, so that became my regular prayer time. If someone was riding with me, I'd explain to him, and we wouldn't talk as we drove. Even though my life is busy, I have to get off to spend time in prayer. Even my wife has to understand this. I have to go away alone at times for a day or two just to pray and be with the Father. The rush of life gets to me. Prayer is a necessity in my life.

One of the great joys of walking with the cross as I do is that I get to pray all the time while I'm walking. I usually walk from five to eight hours a day. That means five to eight hours for prayer along the road. Sometimes I'm having so much fun visiting with the Father that I almost hate to see a car stop. I don't even care to fellowship with Christians walking along with me. Sometimes people will say, "I want to just walk along and talk." Well, if I let them do it, it's so that I can minister to them, but for myself, I'd rather walk alone with the Father.

When you are in prayer, you don't have to talk all the time. And you don't ever have to sign off. Sometimes we sign off with "Amen." Then, later we start again, "It's Arthur Blessitt coming to you now from Hollywood, California." If you're saved and filled with the spirit, then you can pray without ceasing. Even when your mind's on something else, you can be in an attitude of fellowship with God. If you're really close to someone, you don't have to go yak, yak, yak, yak all the time you're with them, do you? If you've got to talk and reassure someone that you love him, it begins to be boring. If you really love him, you can simply be close without talking all the time. It's good to be in quiet communion with God, fellowshiping, visiting with Him, listening to the voice of His Spirit. Many times I don't even feel that I've begun to pray until after I've run out of steam, until I've unloaded everything I need to say and ask. Then, the Lord starts ministering to me. That's when real praying starts.

A Loving Attitude Paves the Way

You are not ready for a life of witness until you are a loving person, inside and out. You may have to take a strong stand on some issues, but it must always be done in love. You need to be a *person* of love.

That doesn't mean you should be a weakling. There's nobody who was any stronger than Jesus, and yet He was a loving person. He was a person of conviction, and yet the overriding emphasis of His life was love. People knew that He loved them. It is in the same way that a non-violent person can be a powerful witness for Jesus Christ.

I've had to prepare the people who minister with us in Hollywood to face some very difficult situations. I have to tell them that they may hear some of the dirtiest language they've ever heard. They may be physically threatened. Their response to such mistreatment will be their most important witness for Jesus Christ. If you are steaming inside, people will sense it. You don't have to say anything. So the most effective way to be sure people won't be coming to you for help is just to resent them inside. They won't come around. But on the other hand, an inner attitude of love will attract more people than you will be able to minister unto.

Jesus Is an Emotional High

If your mood depends on your success in witnessing,

you'll always be up and down. The Bible tells us that one of the fruits of the Spirit is consistency in attitude (Galatians 5:22-23). Such consistency comes from the Holy Spirit, not from success or failure.

If you're up on cloud nine when you lead someone to Jesus, but become despondent and miserable when you don't, you'll never be an effective witness. You'll always be up and down, just depending on whether you have had success or failure. There is no success or failure in evangelism. There is only witnessing and living to serve God. Then as you obey Him, there will be results, there will be fruit, people will be saved. But your life should have the same emotional tone all the time. Isn't it wonderful to know someone who has the same positive attitude whether they're tired, or whether it's early in the morning, or whether circumstances have gone against them? If you're witnessing consistently in a local area, those are the people who will be noticed.

I heard a song on a Christian radio station that I couldn't believe had been written by a believer in Jesus. It talked about the mountains and valleys in life, and thanked God for both kinds of experiences. The song writer said, "I've been in the valleys, so it makes me feel good to go up on the mountains. I couldn't appreciate the ups if I didn't have the downs." In my opinion, that is straight from the devil. It isn't biblical.

Jesus said, "My yoke is easy and my burden is light." (Matthew 11:30). It is *easier* to be a Christian than it is to be a lost person. It is *easier* to live the Christian life than it is to live life for the devil. If you don't believe it, I defy you to come along with us sometime and look at all the people who are lost. Then look at a bunch of really spiritual witnesses for Jesus and tell me which is the happiest group. It's not easy to live with the deep knowledge that you're going to hell. It's not easy to live with the deep knowledge that you're not right with God. It's not easy to live without the Spirit of God. It's abnormal. We were made to have God dwelling in us, and it's abnormal if He's not dwelling in us. It's easier to live life with God.

Suppose you were counseling with someone who had pointed a pistol at his brain. He's in trouble, about to commit suicide. He has dialed the telephone and called your number. He says, "I'm about to die because life is nothing. It's so hard. I've got a .45 magnum at my brain and I'm fixing to blow my brains out. Can you help me?" Suppose you answered, "You think you've got troubles now. Wait 'til you get saved! It's harder to be a Christian than to live for the devil." What's he going to do? Bang! He'll blow his brains out. There's no point in living if it's harder to be a Christian than it is to be a lost person. It's not. It's easier. "My yoke is easy." "The way of the transgressor is hard." "There is no peace for the wicked." There is peace for the righteous, so you live in that peace, that happiness. You live in Jesus. Christianity is an emotional high, not a drag.

Focus on Christ, Not the Devil

Concentrate on Christ in your life, and not on the devil. Some Christians are involved full-time in fighting the devil, always talking about the devil. They're scared of demons and are constantly looking for unclean spirits. They are so used to looking for what's demonic and evil and wicked that their eyes are no longer on Christ. They do not see the glory of God. They cannot appreciate the beauty of people, because all they can see is wickedness. This is not healthy, and cannot lead to a positive witness for Jesus Christ.

Just take a look at Christian television programs. On all the successful ones, the evangelist or teacher focuses on sharing the good news, sharing the victory of life. This is because even the lost don't want to hear about the devil all the time. They want to know about the victory that is in Jesus Christ. So let your vocabulary be full of words about the Lord, and let your thoughts be on Him. Then you will be able to walk right into the middle of the devil's territory without fear. If you're right with God, you don't need to worry at all.

When I was walking through East Africa, I came across big warning signs: STAY IN YOUR CAR—WILD ANIMALS. But I prayed, "God, you made these animals and you made me, and you can keep them from eating me." I hadn't run from anyone, so I wasn't going to let animals scare me off. And none of them bothered me.

We walked right through Northern Ireland, where people warned us, "If you try to go in with all these people, either the IRA will kill you or the Prostestants will kill you." But, we went right through. I spent three and a half months in Northern Ireland, and never had anyone even cuss me out. At one time, I preached to over 200 IRA gunmen at their invitation.

When Billy Graham called and wanted to minister with me over there, I said, "You can come if you don't bring any news media." That was all right, but his people wanted him to have bodyguards with him. I said, "No. He and Sherry (my wife) and I go alone or we don't go at all." They said, "We've got to protect him." I said, "If the British army can't get through without snipers hitting them, you're not going to get Billy through with a bunch of bodyguards. He'll get killed. But if he goes alone, you've nothing to worry about. They're not going to want to kill a couple of unarmed preachers. It wouldn't put points on anyone's merit badge. I'll tell the IRA we're coming, and I'll tell the Protestants." They said, "You mean you'll tell them?" I said, "Sure, I don't want to just spring it on them. I want them to know, and then there won't be any shooting. They'll watch the whole area we're going through." Finally, Billy Graham's people agreed to it.

When he came, I gave Billy a roll of stickers, and I told him to put one on his jacket. He stuck it down a little low, so I told him, "No, no, up here on your chest." He asked, "Why there?" And I said, "Well, if one of the snipers decides to kill you and he sights on the sticker, you'll die right away. If you have the sticker on your stomach, it'll take you all day to die." He put the sticker over his heart and never took it off.

No one bothered us during that walk in Northern Ireland. There was hatred all around, but none of it touched us. You can go right into the devil's territory without fear, if your attention is always on Christ.

Self-Consciousness Is Really Self-Centeredness

If you're going to be an effective witness, you need to get rid of the most subtle kind of self-centeredness—*self-consciousness.* If you are always putting yourself down, that means self is too important in your mind, and you won't be able to share Christ very well.

I was working on Hollywood Boulevard when a Christian lady came up. She had seen our ministry on television, and she was thrilled. She lived right in Hollywood, and she'd been walking with the Lord, so I said, "Why don't you come down and witness with us?" She said, "I can't." I asked why. Do you know what her answer was? "*I'm too fat.* I'm too self-conscious about my weight to witness." Now, she *is* a very large lady, but she was letting that fact control her life. I said, "My, that's a self-pitying excuse. You get your Bible and meet us back here on the sidewalk, and let's go to work for God." She hesitated, so I said, "You're feeling sorry for yourself and running yourself down. Who's in you?" She said, "The Lord." I asked again, "Who? Say it louder." She said, "The Lord!" Then I said, "If you're good enough for God to live in you, you're good enough to tell others about Jesus! Forget whether you're a skinny stringbean or whether you are fat, whether you're short or tall. God loves you; go to work and serve Him."

You'll never be an effective witness for Jesus if you're running yourself down. If you've got the attitude, "I wish I were as good-looking as this other lady, I wish I were as young as her, I wish I was as muscular as him," you are too attached to your own ego. If you feel run down and run over and humiliated and worthless and valueless, you'll never be able to help another person understand that God loves and values him. Now, we do need to be convicted of sin and to repent and get sin out of our lives. We should feel bad about that which is wrong. But, what I'm talking about is something deeper than that—a hatred of yourself, not just your sin.

If you look at yourself as worthless, then you will be worthless in the service of God. Instead, you should look at your body as the temple of God, and feel good about it. "Praise the Lord, thank you God, You live in me." I've got a crooked finger, and when my children are misbehaving and I point and say, "Straighten up now," the children always say, "Daddy, will you use the other finger?" I'm going to have a crooked finger until I meet the Lord. The doctor said that for $500 he could straighten it out, but it wouldn't bend; it would be permanently straight. Well, I'd rather be able to bend it, even though it's crooked. Maybe there are some crooked things in your life that you would like perfected. Don't worry about them. Don't let them keep you from witnessing and sharing Jesus Christ.

Things vs. People

When I was carrying the cross in Africa, I went through an area in Sierra Leone that is one of the richest diamond mining regions in the world. Yet, I was amazed to see the most extreme poverty imaginable. The people were poor and starving, since they lived in the savannah drought belt. The diamonds here are close to the surface, some even lying on the ground. So, people have poured in from all over Africa to find their fortune—tens of thousands of them. They're seeking an escape, a dream, a possible way out of poverty into success.

I walked through the region with my cross, wearing short britches, a T-shirt and boots, and thousands of people followed me. I could preach anytime and have a guaranteed crowd. We gave out Bibles and won many to the Lord.

One day, a Methodist missionary insisted I put down my cross, get into his Land Rover and see the other side of life. He took me to the headquarters of the diamond mining company. Around the compound there was a high barbed wire fence. Patrolling it were soldiers carrying rifles. We drove up to the gate, and since we were the right color, they opened the gate and we drove right on in. They knew the missionary anyway.

The stark contrast that I saw left a lifelong impression on me. Outside was literal starvation and absolute impoverishment. Every inch of dirt in the surrounding hillsides had been dug up in a search for diamonds. People were out there with shovels, hoes and makeshift tools trying to find someway to get out of their misery. And yet inside the compound, behind the fence and behind the patrolling soldiers were a beautiful golf course, a swimming pool, a huge supermarket with all the food you could want from Europe or America. There were doctors, nurses, a hospital, air-conditioned homes, a bar and nightclub, and a movie theater. Every symbol of the same wealth or success that we have in America had been transplanted out there in Sierra Leone right in the middle of the starvation belt.

As I saw it, my heart was grieved. They were glad to see me come. They said, "Well, it's good to have a new preacher around. Will you preach for us tonight? We'll get everyone together in the bar and lounge area and you can speak to us." I'm always witnessing but that afternoon I didn't witness at all. I just listened to try to understand their minds. I knew I'd have a captive audience that evening, and I wanted to be on target. I listened to big groups of whites and the handful of Sierra Leonian blacks who were living inside the compound. The night when I got up to speak, I think I was more burdened than I've ever been in my life while sharing a message to a group of people. I stood up, and tears started streaming down my cheeks. I said to them, "Men and ladies, I want you to know that you are blind, you are blind. You hate these jungles, you hate these rocks, you hate the malaria, you hate the tse-tse fly, you hate being here. The only thing that's brought you here is these little rocks that sparkle. You are blind, because the only thing in Sierra Leone of any value at all is not the diamonds. The only thing of any value is the people, the men, the women, the children. Those little children have swollen bellies because of malnutrition. And you've been blinded by the attraction of little rocks. The only thing that is of value is the people."

I want you to know that there are many attractive and sparkling things that can hold your attention and your mind and your energy in America today. There is every sort of recreation imaginable, there is every sort of thrill you can conceive of, every kind of sensation you could imagine. But, I tell you, the only real value in the world is people—be it the governor or a prostitute, the impoverished or the rich, the only value is people. God so loved the world, God so loved the people, that He gave His only begotten Son for us. He sent Jesus for people, not to save the rivers or the streams. Jesus didn't come to die for the snow-capped mountains or the beautiful valleys. He died for people who have rebelled against their Creator and need to be saved. And He said, "As the Father has sent me, so send I you" (John 20:21). Our hearts must throb with His love for people, and that's why we should reach out to share Jesus with everyone.

That diamond mining company had set up a fence, separating those on the inside from those on the outside. I said, "Thank you Lord, there's no fence with you. You haven't erected a barrier; you love all. Whosoever will may come, and drink of the water of life freely. God's diamonds are for everybody. God's diamonds are free. Jesus paid it all. All to Him I owe. Sin has left a crimson stain, but Jesus washes white as snow." He has His diamonds for you. You may look at someone whose dress or behavior or vocabulary is exactly the opposite of what you think it should be. But, God loves them. They're God's diamonds, and Jesus is seeking to save them. He wants to reach them because He loves them. He wants their stomachs full, He wants their wounds bound up, He wants their loneliness cured, He wants their guilt erased, He wants them to have hope, He wants to wipe away the tears and give them joy. He's interested in where you live and in what kind of clothes you wear. God's interested in everything, the very hairs of your head are numbered. God is interested in people, and therefore our interest must be in people. They are not vague souls that need to be saved. They are not figures that are moving up and down the freeway. They are human beings like you and me, with the same needs. God wants to give them all of His blessings, just as He does for you.

Jesus told a story about a shepherd who counted his sheep to see that all were safely in the sheepfold. But he found that one was missing. He left the 99, and he went out and searched until he had found that one that was lost. He did not rest until he had found that one that needed him. Our call in life is to move through the streets and roadsides, and through the businesses and the schools and everywhere else we go, to find those that are lost and bring them into the family of the Father.

When you do this, some may feel that you are being radical. But if there's a fire burning in a house, and you know there are people in it, you will explode into action even if you're a mild-mannered person. You won't just park the car and knock softly on the door so as not to disturb anyone. You become a raging fanatic, and people accept it as normal, because you're trying to save them from dying. You wake them up and you get them out of the house. Well, the world is on fire, and people are being snatched into destruction moment by moment. We've got to reach out and share with them the living good news.

Many years ago, a wise, old priest lived in a mountain

monastery in Greece. A young priest came to him one day with a problem. "I've been trying to carry out the commands of Jesus, and live like our Lord and Master, but people are laughing at me. They're joking about me and calling me abnormal. I find it hard to be like Jesus and to be considered normal by the people in my parish." The old priest told him a story that happened in Jerusalem. Now, you'll be sure that he made it up because it's such a strange story, but here it is.

"There was a temple priest in Jerusalem who had special power from God. He was able to deal with people who were unbalanced or abnormal and correct them so that they were normal. People were brought to him for prayer and counsel. A man and woman once brought their young son to him. The boy's name was Jesus. They said they were having all kinds of problems with him. He wanted to teach and preach in the temple without even telling his parents where he was going. He was very abnormal, wanting to talk about the Kingdom of God all the time. He wasn't like all the other boys in the town of Nazareth where they lived and they wanted to see if there was anything that the priest could do with him. The priest said, 'Let me keep him for a month.' After a month, Mary and Joseph came back and took Jesus back home. He was just as normal as can be. The last anyone ever heard of him was he was the best carpenter in Nazareth." The young priest got the message. He went back down to live like Jesus.

You see, if Jesus had been normal you wouldn't be here today. He would have been like every other little boy in Israel. But he wasn't. If you are His follower, you're not going to be normal either. I hope you let your normality be judged by Jesus, and not by the community around you.

Sometimes I've gotten complaints about all the stickers and tracts that show up along Hollywood Boulevard. My answer is, "We'll quit giving out tracts and stickers if you'll clear up all the filthy, dirty books that are on all the stands. If you'll remove all those offensive porno newsstands all down the sidewalk, if you'll shut down all the porno stores, if you get rid of all that filth, then I'll gladly quit printing stickers. But until then, Praise the Lord, we're going to keep passing them out. And if someone litters the sidewalk by throwing a tract down, Praise God. People are always throwing all kinds of dirty magazines on the pavement." We are disciples of Jesus and it is our aim to be like Him. That's not considered normal in this world.

There's only a fine line between a saint and an insane person. It's no wonder that people can't tell the difference. Both the saint and the insane person are dealing in the abnormal; they're both dealing with another world. The insane man is always talking about things the average person can't see, and so is the saint. His life is full of things that can't be seen by the eye. He is always talking about God working and God doing miracles and God changing lives. To the average person, it sounds like he's talking about outer space. Sometimes he may be labeled as crazy. And the more spiritual he becomes, the more insane he appears to be. Anyone who starts living like Jesus will have to accept that kind of misunderstanding.

Even Jesus had to put up with this kind of reaction. The people who saw His miracles said He was doing them in the name of Beelzebub, the devil. Jesus is God, and here they were saying that He is the devil. It shouldn't be too surprising then if the more you become like Jesus, the more some people will think you're of the devil.

That's why on the day of Pentecost, when the disciples were filled with the Spirit, the people thought they were drunk. They were abnormal. They weren't behaving like the normal person in Jerusalem on that day so the people figured something must be wrong with them. If you go around happy, people will swear that you take acid, or stay high on grass, or pop pills. They'll say, "No one can stay up that long and be that happy without turning on to something." They can't understand that being high is normal for a Christian.

Do You Have Time for Your Family?

When you become involved in a witnessing ministry, especially if it involves night work, you've got to be very conscious of your family's needs. It's usually the wife who is constantly stuck at home caring for the children. If the husband is always going out to help others, she sooner or later begins to resent the fact that he's never around to help her.

Sherry and I have had a good time ministering together, even with the children. Our five children have all been involved in ministry with us, and I can't see that they've been hurt at all. We had Gina out when she was a teeny bitty baby, bundled up against the cold in Nevada. Joseph has been carried around the world, and he's still kicking. Joshua grew up in constant contact with the world. You can take your children with you in ministry, but you can't take them all the time. They've got to go to school much of the year, and sometimes they'll be sick. So that means you're going to be out alone a lot.

Some families have a problem because the wife is very possessive in the relationship. She has never had any trouble trusting her husband, and suddenly he's staying out all night. He comes in and she asks, "Where have you been?" "Well, I took this prostitute across town because she was drunk." "Well, what were you doing *there?*" Once this kind of pattern begins, the trust in the marriage is undermined. I've seen homes destroyed by this problem.

It's the person who's left at home that has the hardest time. It's not nearly so bad for the one who is out working. He can say, "Have supper ready at 7:00," and then get involved in helping someone and be out until 6:00 the next morning. But his wife just waits hour after hour after hour. This happens over and over again, and one day she doesn't make supper. That's the day he comes home on time, and now there's a war going.

Another pressure on your family is that your home can

easily become an extension of your ministry. You want to be available so you say, "Come over or call any time." And they do. Every time you sit down to eat, the phone rings and rings. You stay out all night and when you come in, someone is waiting to eat breakfast with you, besides your wife. You go to sleep after a night's work, and you wake up at 1:00 in the afternoon. You look up and there are ten people sitting in the living room ready to visit you. "We've been waiting for you, Praise the Lord." Before long, you are going day after day, and you're never alone with your children. You're never alone with your wife. You're never even alone with yourself. Your home becomes a motel, with nothing personal about it at all.

Now, it's good to reach the point where there are many people wanting your help. But then you will probably have to reach another point, the point where you have to say, "Don't come to my house, don't come and visit. I need to have some time with my family." Don't call on the telephone. Just sit around all afternoon in peace and quiet.

If you have children, you must spend time with them. If you don't, they're going to find someone who will. If they don't have a good time with Daddy, then they're going to have a good time with something else. If it takes acid for them to have that good time, they'll turn to acid. So you've got the choice of either spending time with them all along the way or regretting it for years of agony and heartache. You need to spend quality time with your family, just with them.

Worn Out Tools Don't Do Good Work

We really need to be fresh in order to do our best work for Jesus Christ. The Lord will use us in spite of our physical weakness for a short period of time if there's nothing we can do to avoid the circumstance. There are times when I extend myself far beyond what I would normally be doing, but it's because there's a crisis at hand. There are nights when I work right through till morning because of some special needs. But that can't be my continual pattern, or I'll lose my effectiveness.

It's good to have a protective environment you can escape to. Mine is my home. My wife, Sherry, knows when I need to sleep late, when the phone should be unplugged, when to turn visitors away.

One practice that's helped me is to take an extra day at the end of the month of crusades or rallies before I come home. I spend that day sleeping. If I were to come straight home, the kids would want to play. "Daddy, Daddy, Daddy, let's go here, let's go eat out." I've *been* eating out, I've *been* running. So it's better for me to stay an extra day and get a day and night's sleep. Then I can come home to my family rested, wide awake and ready to enjoy them. If you don't do something like this, you'll always come dragging in, and that's not good for the family situation.

Sometimes, I'll schedule a day off after a period of going strong and hard. I may get in at 4:00 in the morning and sleep till noon. Then I'll roll out of bed, get a bite to eat, and go back to bed again. I just sleep and store up energy all day long.

No one can be involved in ministry 24 hours a day. You have to figure out your kind of ministry. If you stay out all night, then you need to sleep all morning. It doesn't matter when you get your sleep, but somehow you need to get the same amount of rest that you normally would. When I'm carrying the cross during the day, I don't usually do much at night. Most often, I'm in bed an hour after I've finished the day's walk. I'm exhausted physically, and I have to have a full night's sleep. I'm exhausted and then I need to go to sleep. And when I am really worn out, I go to sleep even during the day. If there's any way, then I find that the Lord will let me do it, even though I've gone to sleep. I've lain down and gone to sleep when there were hundreds of people standing around wanting me to preach. If they come in, I'll preach a brief message and have to go to sleep because I may have walked 30 miles that day with a 90 pound cross, and my body is done in. I share a brief message and then tell them, "I'll preach to you more at breakfast," and I lie down.

The Secret of Relaxation

Not only does an effective witness need to get enough sleep, but he also has to learn to have a relaxed attitude about life. When you learn to *live relaxed,* it doesn't matter how fast things are popping around, you've got double the strength. Sometimes I have people working with me at rallies and crusades keeping me on schedule and helping me get my work done. They'll go with me for three days, and then they're dead tired. But I may leave there and go to another crusade. I may wear out 15 or 20 people, one after the other, and I'm still going strong, because I am relaxed. I'm not running around full of tension. When your muscles are tense and you're tied up, you burn energy. But when you live relaxed, you save energy. Your mind is at rest, you're sharp, you're effective. But if you're all tensed up, tied up, knotted, you aren't going to attract many people to Jesus. Look at yourself in the mirror sometime.

I've seen people who are always tensed and tied up in knots. It looks like they've got handcuffs around their throat, their face, their hands, everything. They're just burning unnecessary energy. They're full of tension. You need to learn to rest in the Lord and have peace in your soul. There's no merit in fizzing, just standing there like a bomb ready to explode. Save your energy. If you're not going anywhere, stand still and relax.

If you're full of tension, you can wear yourself out just riding thirty minutes to work. But if your mind is at rest and at peace in the Lord, that same ride can be a refreshing experience, even if the traffic is terrible. A traffic jam can make a spiritual spastic of you, but if you rest in the Lord you can fight off life's tensions.

Don't Be Afraid of Hard Work

There is a time for rest and relaxation, but there is also a time for good, honest hard work for the Lord.

You ought to do a good job for God. A person goes out and works eight hours a day digging ditches or pouring cement, or pushing papers in an office. And if you're in a full-time ministry, you ought to put in some solid hours for God. Don't mind working for the Lord, and don't even back away from doing physical work.

I feel better when I'm walking with the cross than I do at other times because when I'm physically exerting myself, I'm stronger in every other way as well. After a few weeks of walking with the cross, I have to start exercising again, running, doing push-ups, etc. Your body needs a good physical burning out; it needs a good sweating. So don't mind working for the Lord. If you have to wash dishes to make a living so you can witness at night, do it with enthusiasm. Whatever you do, do it well, because that's part of your Christian witness.

Success May Be Failure

Be careful not to fall into the trap of gimmick evangelism and addiction to numbers. Many ministries lose their spirited power when they begin to play the numbers game. If there is one area where the cult of success is totally out of place, it is in Christian ministry. But many leaders treat Christianity much like McDonald's hamburgers. You always look at a McDonald's restaurant to see how many more billion hamburgers have been sold. Tick, tick, tick, tick, tick—each number change means one more hamburger has been eaten. Now, having a desire to see people saved is good. But you've got to be careful. Before long you'll start counting the converts. You'll start publishing a little sheet on how many you led to the Lord this month. Of course, the next month, there has to be an increase. The third month it may be way down. You may have 75 saved one month and 150 the next month. But then it may drop to 35 the next. You don't want to put that 35 in your newsletter. It looks like you weren't spiritual that month, and that's why the number of converts was down. You may even begin to exaggerate a little bit, because you've caught the success fever.

Some Christian ministries are always spouting numbers, numbers, numbers. I have the feeling that God is sick of it. I know it turns me off and it does most non-Christians as well. People aren't just numbers; they're human beings.

The numbers game can lead to a lot of frustration and dissatisfaction. You may have 500 attending your meeting one Sunday. The next Sunday you drop to 495 so you start a big drive to get over 500 again. You can't even rest. You can't even enjoy being in the house of God without feeling guilty. "We were 500 last week. Got to get ten more than we had last week. We'll give you a super burger if you'll bring somebody. You'll win a bicycle if you get someone saved. You'll be given a free trip to Israel if . . ." And before long, the poor people are only pawns in a big chess game played by Christians trying to reach another record.

Our whole Christian movement is caught up in this numbers game. You can read a Christian magazine and find a score card on churches—which ones give the most money, which have the highest attendance. I've heard preachers that say, "Our church is only number twenty-four on the score card, and we want to move up. We ought to be number one." I want to ask, "Number one what?" You ought to be the church or the evangelist that God wants you to be, and let that be your witness. You're not in a rat race, competing with everyone else.

I've been in it. There was a time years ago when I was caught up in the whole success game. My motives were pure, but I was treating people as numbers. I printed the number of conversions in a monthly newsletter. Then one month the number dropped, so we changed the count from conversions to decisions. That made the number bigger and more impressive.

A preacher gets all kinds of mailings. He reads in one evangelist's literature that he is having about twenty-five conversions each month. Another claims 250 each month. He says, "Our church is about dead; I'd better call up this guy who has 250 a month." So, for the evangelist, the number of conversions gets to be a kind of scorecard by which he is rated.

In my street ministry, I have deliberately avoided talking about how many have been led to the Lord. There will be some weeks in which very few are led to Christ, and there will be others when there are a lot of conversions. That doesn't say anything about your witnessing. You're probably just as right with God this week as you were last week or will be next week. There's no reason for you to feel guilty or intimidated when results are lower, or to feel that you deserve a merit badge when they're higher. You can see how childish and unspiritual all this sounds, and yet much Christian ministry is run that way.

I praise God for everyone who is saved. I'd rather win 20 a day to Jesus than one a day, wouldn't you? But it's wrong to be constantly aware of numerical success. It robs you of the peace of mind and the relaxed attitude that produces the best Christian witness.

11

The Holy Spirit and Witnessing

Filled with the Spirit

The Bible encourages us to "be filled with the Spirit" (Ephesians 5:18), and if you're going to witness for Jesus you'd better be sure you have that filling first. In witnessing, you need to be directed by the Spirit of God as to where to go, what to do, and what to say. If you're not Spirit-filled, then you'll just be talking in the flesh. Sometimes God will use the words anyway, but He can't use you as effectively as He could if you were filled with His Spirit and under His control.

The purpose of the filling of the Holy Spirit is not to make you feel good. It isn't just to give you a bunch of spiritual toys to play with—called "gifts." Some people seem to be saying, "I'm filled with the Spirit, and I've got this gift. What have you got?" So whole groups of Christians are standing around, saying, "Gee, that looks nice; I think I'll have a little of that, and one of these, Lord, and a couple of these. Gimme, gimme, gimme." This is not Spirit filling, but a bunch of self-righteous people indulging themselves.

The filling of the Holy Spirit is designed to *give you power in witnessing and victory in living.* When you have victory in living and power in witnessing, then Praise God, you *do* feel good, and Praise God, there are gifts that He gives. But that is not the purpose of the filling; that is not the reason. The reason is to give you the power *to do something.* There are many people who say, "I'm filled with the Spirit," but they haven't begun to act the way the Christians acted on the day of Pentecost. Some people say,

"I've received the Spirit," and they can speak in tongues for six hours straight, yet they haven't ever gone out on the street and preached. They've focused on one little aspect of something that happened, and they haven't seen the big picture. God filled them with the Spirit so they could go out on the streets and preach.

When those first Spirit-filled Christians preached on the streets of Jerusalem, people were saved—3,000 of them the first day. This happened because they *got filled and got out.* They didn't sit around sharing with one another how wonderful the filling was, they went out and shared it with the world. They communicated a simple, powerful message that people could understand and identify with. They explained that they were lost and that Jesus could save them. People today are just as hungry and responsive to that simple message shared by Spirit-filled Christians.

There's something wrong when you can get thrilled in a meeting but you can't get thrilled outside the door. We get so excited about Jesus when we're with a group of Christians. We see everybody praising God, 500 in a rally, souped up and praising the Lord. Then, they walk out the door. Shhh! They put their Bibles under their coats, their lips are sealed. These "hallelujah Christians" go into a restaurant and a lost waitress serves them. They sit there eating pie and praising God for the rally, but that woman serves them, puts napkins on the table, takes their menus, does everything but kiss them, and they never even think about sharing Christ with her. Something's wrong with that kind of Christianity. Now, I'm not saying there's anything wrong with praising the Lord, but brother, they need it in the restaurant, they need it at the laundromat, they need it on the streets. If the power of Christ doesn't reach these places, it's an abortion of spirituality. It's something that starts but is never finished.

So, Spirit filling and witnessing have to go together. Witnessing without Spirit-filling is hollow; Spirit filling without witnessing is incomplete.

Called by the Spirit

When God wants someone to do a job for Him, He calls that person by His Holy Spirit. It's not easy to describe what a call from God is like, but He knows how to get His message through to us in unmistakable ways.

When you know that God is leading you into a ministry, you'd better do it. If you don't, you'll never be the same. That is a warning. God will forgive you, but you'll never reach the spiritual state that God wants you to be in, and that is an awesome kind of failure. If there's anything that I'm concerned about in my life, it's to be ready to do what God wants me to do. I don't want to get out of step with His will even once.

I could tell you story after story after story about people whom God called. He laid right before them an opportunity that was ready to explode; but they hesitated, they waited, and that opportunity went by. Because they didn't respond to His call, God raised up someone else. The ones who did not obey the call may be living for the Lord, praising God, loving Jesus. God may be using them, but they know that they'll never be where they could have been with God.

I can give you illustrations of people I've been involved with personally who hesitated when God called. God was ready to go with them, but they weren't. Two months later they were ready, but the opportunity was passed. Since then, they've continued with the Lord, but they've never been as effective as they could have been if they'd answered the call then.

Don't you play games with God's will. Don't take His call lightly. I don't know whether this is theologically sound, but I think God will have more mercy on someone who's *trying* to follow His call, even if he sometimes stumbles along doing it, than on someone who never responds to His call. You look at the examples in the Bible. When God chose someone, He often put up with a lot of foolishness. He judged them, He dealt with them, but as long as they were trying to follow Him, as long as they were preaching, as long as they were doing what God called them to do, God's armor was over them. Even when they were wrong, God was still with them. He endured their petty little whims and straightened them out and disciplined them, but His loving hand was on them. However, if they ever got out of doing what God called them to do, He came down on them hard. You have to face an awesome judgment of God when you turn away from moving the way God wants you to move.

Many people hesitate to answer God's call because they're afraid they won't be able to do what He's asking them to do. But that shouldn't stop you. Just recognize the fact that *no one* can do *anything* for God in his own strength. "It's not by might, by power, but by my Spirit," said the Lord. It's not *you* that does anything, it's not *me* that does anything. It's *God*. You do not convict a person of his sin. You do not convert anyone, you do not save anyone; it's all the Lord. You are just an instrument in His hand to use as He will. When you try to convict, it's self. When you try to convert, it's self. When you just allow the Spirit of God to convict, to convince, to convert, to seal, then you have no hesitation in your ministry.

Someone may look at the ministry you're involved in and say, "Isn't that a pitiful failure?" But it's not their estimation that counts. It's whether you're doing what God tells you to do. It may be that you have been pastor of a big, successful church, but God calls you to a little congregation out in the mountains somewhere. And everyone says, "You're blowing it. You had a great ministry, and you're giving it up." Don't worry about it. You do what God tells you to do. The best place in the world to be is in the will of God. That's the most enjoyable and the happiest place. Let His will come together in your life. Don't worry. If you're in the Father's will, He's going to look after you. He knows your needs. Just minister in triumph. You may be surrounded with failure and frustration, but concentrate on what Jesus is doing and He'll use you.

Led by the Spirit

The call of God is to a specific ministry. This kind of message from the Holy Spirit may come several times in a person's life, at special moments of decision. But the *leading* of the Holy Spirit is a daily, minute-by-minute experience of the Spirit-filled Christian.

Many believers talk about being filled with the Spirit in the past tense. "Yes, I was filled with the Spirit in 1969." But the fact that you were filled with the Spirit in 1969 or in 1976 or last Sunday does not mean that you are full of the Holy Spirit today. And it does not mean that you are led by the Spirit in your life moment by moment right now. If you've been saved, the Holy Spirit is indwelling your life. He is still present with you. But there is a difference between *having* the Holy Spirit in your life and being *led* and *filled* with the Spirit on a day-by-day, moment-by-moment basis. Looking back on past experiences will not give you power for the present.

When you are filled with the Spirit in the present, you are led by the Spirit. He controls your mind, and thoughts and actions, so that your life becomes His life. When you are Spirit-filled, every desire you have is His desire, and along with the desire is the power to perform it. Therefore, there can never be any frustration when you are Spirit-filled.

Many times Christians get desires and ideas for things they want to do for God, but they don't originate in the Spirit of God. That's why they can't accomplish what they want to. This leads to confusion, but God's not the author of confusion; He's the author of harmony and peace. When you are led by the Spirit, and are a spirit-filled person, you will not have to battle in your mind, day-by-day, moment-by-moment—"Is this my will, or is it God's will?"

Putting Out the Fleece

I meet Christians who are so anxious about knowing God's will that their lives are just a series of spiritual nervous breakdowns. They are in spiritual confusion. They may feel a desire to do something, to witness to somebody, and then they start analyzing whether they should or they shouldn't, or what the person would do if they talked to them, or what someone else would think of them. They mull it over, "I wonder if it's my desire to talk to them, or if it's God's desire." So, to deal with their confusion they decide to go back to the signs-and-wonders approach. I am not a signs-and-wonders, will-of-God Christian. That leads to more confusion.

There are Christians who won't move unless God gives them some miraculous sign, unless there is some dramatic event proving to them that it's the will of God. A person may say, "I feel that God wants me in New York to do a certain task." He may feel very strongly that this is the will of God. But, then he begins to think it out, and he says, "Well, if it is God's will, I'd better look for a sign. Maybe the plane ticket. If it's the will of God, then somebody'll come up and give me a plane ticket, and if no one gives me a plane ticket, I'm not going. Lord, send me a plane ticket." Once you begin thinking like this, you'll question everything. "If they want me in New York, somebody'll come up and give me a credit card," or "They'll call me within three hours and ask me." Or maybe you'll have an impulse to go, but you don't know whether it's to New York or Chicago, and you'll say, "Well, Lord, I'll go to either city, just send me a plane ticket in the mail today." And you go to the mail and there are two plane tickets, one for each city! You're still in a state of confusion.

There is one passage in the Old Testament that people use to determine the will of God (Judges 6:36-40). It tells how Gideon put out a fleece over night. Whether or not the fleece was wet in the morning showed him God's will.

Many Christians live their lives by putting out fleeces all over the place. They think that's how the Spirit is leading them.

But Gideon was not demonstrating faith by putting out the fleece; he was showing a doubting spirit. God had already indicated that He wanted Gideon to lead the people to victory, but Gideon was having second thoughts. His faith was wavering. He didn't know any more after the fleece episode than before. God just underlined what His will was, but He didn't reveal anything new.

If you start living your life by laying out fleeces, your Christian life will be in a turmoil. No one will be able to live with you, and you'll even find it hard to live with yourself. Forget the fleece. If God says you should go to New York, go to New York. And if a plane ticket doesn't come in the mail, drive. If you don't have the gas money, hitchhike. If nobody will give you a ride, walk. If you can't walk it, crawl. Die obeying God's will. But do what God tells you to do.

Looking for Open Doors

Another way Christians complicate the Spirit's leading is by always waiting for open doors. Usually, the people who think this way are also the ones who are not doing anything! They're "going to" Christians. They're always on the verge of a miracle, but the miracles never seem to happen because the doors are closed. They're constantly praying, "God, open the door." I don't believe any doors need to be opened. I believe the door is *already open.* The door was opened when Jesus died on the cross. Satan was defeated, and the door was thrown open. If you're doing what God wants you to do and something gets in your way, if it looks like there's a closed door, knock it down, kick your way through it, just keep going. The door is already open. When you obey God, you'll find every door is open. You won't have to open it. Just go ahead and do what God says to do.

It doesn't matter what it costs, or what it looks like. If God says to do it, do it.

If I laid out fleeces, if I waited for open doors, I would not be here today. I would not even have gotten out of town with the cross, and I certainly wouldn't have gone all over the world. I tell you there hasn't been one continent that's invited me to come yet. Nobody invited me to Hollywood to minister on Sunset Strip. As a matter of fact, I had a car wreck on the way, got hit in the head with a bed spring, and ran into all kinds of other obstacles. I could have interpreted them as signs, but I firmly believed that God had said, "Go." So, I went.

When I was about to begin carrying the cross, I ended up in the hospital with a stroke. The doctors said I needed total rest, but God said, "Walk." I walked. I was just trying to do what He told me to do. If I had looked at the state of my body or had listened to what people told me, I wouldn't have even begun.

I can't think of one great thing that I've ever done, not one single great thing. My life is a series of simple little things God has told me to do. People see all these little things piled up, and it looks like something great has happened. But I've just talked to one person about Jesus, and he's been saved, talked to another person over here, and so forth. A series of little acts of obedience adds up to a lifetime of obedience.

So, when the Holy Spirit tells you to do something, *do it.* Don't wait for the big things to happen; follow Him in the little things.

God's Leading May Be Surprising

Two of us were driving home one night in Hollywood. My friend was driving, and I was practically asleep. Suddenly, I was wide awake. The Holy Spirit gave me a picture in my mind of a guy looking out of a second story window. I could see him in profile; his head was down and he was either reading or writing.

I shocked my friend by saying, "Stop, turn left." He didn't know what was happening, but he did it. I kept directing him, "Turn here. Down this street." I had shared my mental picture with my friend, and when we came to a certain point on Santa Monica Boulevard, he said, "There it is; there it is." He was right. Through a second floor window, over a laundromat, I saw the man the Holy Spirit had put in my mind.

My friend said, "What do we do now?" I said, "We're going to knock on the door and lead him to Jesus." I found the door entrance, and knocked. The guy asked, "Who is it?" I said, "It's a preacher. God sent me by to share with you about Jesus." He opened the door. I said, "I was driving down the street, and the Lord told me to come see you." We started talking and he gave his heart to the Lord. He was really ready to be saved. This kind of thing doesn't happen to me often, but when I have a spontaneous impulse from the Spirit, I'm careful to follow it.

I believe God gave me a lesson about following the Holy Spirit when I was a child. I lived on a cotton plantation in Louisiana. My dad would have me carry water to the people who were chopping cotton. I would load up a couple of buckets with ice water and walk through the hot fields. The workers would drink all the ice water, and then I'd take the empty buckets back about an hour later. I'd do it all over again. Quite often I didn't feel like walking out there in the hot sun. I'd walk along like a typical lazy little boy who has to do something he doesn't want to do.

One time I was dragging along when the Lord told me in my heart to turn right. I did. Then He told me to turn left, and I obeyed. Then He told me to take 25 steps in another direction, turn and take 50 steps in another direction. I was zigzagging all over that field. I ended up far from the workers, so my dad drove up in his truck. "What are you doing over here?" "Daddy, God's been telling me to zigzag," I answered. "He said to go 30 steps this way, 20 steps that way." My dad looked at me and said, "I don't care who's telling you what. You get over there with those buckets." By the time I got to the workers, I was crying.

I believe that episode was God's way of giving me a little obedience training. He wanted me to learn to follow His leading without question—whether it seems logical or not, even if others don't understand me. My ministry in the last few years has been a lot like zigzagging over the fields of the world. I don't have any grand strategy. I just follow what the Holy Spirit tells me to do every day.

When There's No Clear Leading

There are many times when the Holy Spirit doesn't reveal what the next step is. When I feel that God is preparing me for something else, but I'm not sure what the direction is, I don't get into a fizz over it. I just wait to see His will unfold in my life.

When you're in the process of discerning the will of God, don't sit in limbo. When you're in doubt, do what the Bible tells you to do. I have people coming to me all the time saying, "I don't know what the will of God for my life is. I don't know what the Lord wants me to do. I don't know whether He wants me over here, or over there." And while they're waiting to find out, they're usually doing absolutely nothing.

You may not know where God wants you next, but you can work for Him where you are right now. Share the love of Jesus, be involved in witnessing, feed the poor, love the lonely. There is more work than you can handle right where you are. So do it, now, and then when God reveals some other place to minister you'll be ready to do the same thing there. The only thing that really matters is that you do God's will wherever you are. It's His will for you to minister all the time.

A lot of people come up to me and say, "I want to join you and walk with you." And boy, they're ready to explode; they're ready to go. I say, "What's your ministry right now?" Well, I tell you, I'm in school now," or "I've got a job that keeps me busy, but boy, if I could quit this and join you full time I'd really be turned on for Jesus." You know, if I needed help, it sure wouldn't be from that kind of person, because he's not doing anything now. If you don't have enough oomph to witness now, how are you going to do it when you go somewhere else? Sure, you can get caught up in the excitement and get started, but pretty soon things will get tough and you'll just fall over flat.

If there's ever any question as to what you should be doing or where you should be going, then just do what you know God wants His followers to do—go into all the world and make disciples. Keep doing that and the will of God will become clear. The more you're involved in the service of God, the clearer the will of God for your life becomes.

Peace of Mind and Heart

I usually feel peace in my life, and when I don't, when I feel restless, I've learned to take this as a sign of God's leading me.

My family and I were in Paris on our way across Europe. This was during the time I was carrying the cross around the world. We were starting out for Munich, but I had only taken a few steps when I suddenly felt restless and had no peace. I stopped dead in my tracks and I stood there a second. I pulled out my map of Europe and opened it. I followed the map toward Munich, and I had no peace. I looked at Scandinavia and at Holland—no peace. I traced the map toward Rome, and there was still no peace.

There was one other direction—toward Spain. That wasn't going to help me go around the world because it was in the wrong direction. Besides, Spain was the only place where I had no contacts. Yet, as I looked at the map of Spain, I felt God's peace.

I went over to my wife, Sherry, in the van and I showed her the map. "Look, we can go this way, or this way, or this way. Or, we could go to Spain." Sherry started crying, and she said, "Arthur, God's been burdening my heart, but I haven't said a word about it. He's been telling me that we ought to go to Africa." And through Spain is the way to Africa.

From that moment, we knew in our hearts that God was going to send an awakening to Spain, and we felt peace as we started out in that direction.

Never Look Back

It didn't look much like an awakening at first. Gary Davis, a Baptist pastor, traveled with me as interpreter. He was all spruced up, with a suit and tie, so I rumpled up his hair a bit. He asked what I was doing. I answered, "I'm loosening you up. If you're going with me, you've got to be loose."

We crossed the border and gave out stickers and tracts. We preached to hundreds of people along the street. But we had only gone about a mile when the police came. We were both arrested and thrown into jail.

So, we sat in jail for a day. I might have thought, "Well, Arthur, I guess you made a mistake in Paris. If you'd have kept going you'd still be preaching." But, I didn't. I never even thought in that direction. I never look back. I don't do anything, if in my soul I don't feel it's right, and after I've decided to do it, I don't look back. I don't ever say, "If I had made the other decision this might not have happened." I say, "Glory to God, as best as I knew how, I made the decision God was leading me to make." In that jail I was thinking and praying, "Now, God, how are you going to use this, lead me as to how to make the greatest witness possible."

While we were in jail the one day, Gary suddenly said, "Hey, Arthur, I'm loose!" He was remembering the incident when I rumpled his hair. But his words also symbolized for me the feeling of confidence we have when we have peace about being led by God's Spirit and in the center of His will.

The Holy Spirit and Reason

It's true that the Holy Spirit may lead us in ways that don't seem reasonable, but if we could see all the facts we would realize that the Spirit and reason are always in harmony. There isn't a thing that I've ever done in my life that has not been logical and reasonable in some sense. Now, let me illustrate this. If I only have a few dollars, enough to put a down payment on something, but not enough for me to be sure I can pay it off, I don't spiritualize the issue and buy it, trusting God for the payments. If I did, I would have a huge pile of debts lying on top of me. When I start out on a trip with my wife and kids, our action may not seem logical. It may sound totally weird to everyone else in the world, but in my mind, it is perfectly reasonable. We may have only $500, but I know if we're careful, spending only a few dollars a day, we can make it to our destination. I don't check in at the Hilton just because I've got $500, and then come to God saying, "Lord, you've abandoned us out here." No, I feel responsible to use my reason so that the resources He's given me will go as far as possible.

Some Christian ministers feel that to be led by the Spirit means to do things that are illogical. So they jump impulsively into impossible situations and then they expect God to bail them out. We should follow the leading of God's Spirit, but we need to keep our reason in gear all the time. Both the Spirit and our reason are gifts from God. They work best in harmony.

The Holy Spirit and Money

The fact that I am following the Spirit's leading does not give me the right to go around begging. One of the worst things a person in a ministry can get into is the telling of sad, sad stories about his financial problems. If there's anything that makes me sick, it's to hear someone in Christian ministry moaning about not having any money. My wife, kids, and I ate day-old bagels and pastries on Sunset

Strip during the fall of 1967 and all of 1968. We had nothing. We ate the leftover food that we'd get from catering services, and bakeries. When people asked me, "How are you making it, Brother Blessitt?" I'd say, "Just fine, Praise the Lord."

If you're not careful, you'll develop a ministry with such an overhead of expenses that you're working most of the time just to produce the money to survive. Then you'll have to have crowds just to raise income. And, you'll be laying burden after burden on them. You've got to raise that money, because you have thousands of dollars in debts every month. Before you know it, you've become very commercialized. Everything is money, money, money.

That's why I travel light. I don't have a staff, because if I did I'd have to go out preaching just to make the money to pay them. That would be prostituting for Jesus. I cannot preach for money—I do it only to do God's will. I can't begin to think, "Is this a big church or a little church? Will there be a good offering?"

Because I don't beg for money, a lot of people think I'm a millionaire. That's O.K. As a matter of fact, anyone with good, healthy pride would rather have people think he is loaded than to be reduced to begging for money.

Make sure the money issue is always in the background. God's Spirit has called you to a ministry. The money is only a way to accomplish that ministry. Don't get into obligations you can't afford. God will bless you with the finances you need if you handle them carefully and humbly.

Prepare to Share Jesus

Now I'd like you to go through the entire way of salvation with another Christian. Ask him to respond to you as if he were lost. This will be a very helpful exercise in preparing you for a life of sharing Jesus.

The Last Word

You may have read this book to the last page and still not know Jesus. I invite you to pray this prayer right now:

> Dear God, have mercy on me and forgive my sins. Jesus, come into my heart and save me now. I want You in my life forever. Make my home heaven, and fill me with Thy love and Thy Holy Spirit. Thank You, Lord. In Jesus' name. Amen."

If you would like more information or help, please write:

Arthur Blessitt Evangelical Association
P.O. Box 69544
Hollywood, CA 90069

THE NEW LIFE TRACT SCRIPTURE REFERENCES

- Jesus has come to live within your heart.
  Revelation 3:20

- Your sins are forgiven.
  1 John 1:7-9; 2 Peter 3:9

- You are saved.
  Romans 10:9-13

- You have received eternal life.
  John 3:16; Romans 6:23

- You are now the child of God.
  John 1:12; Ephesians 2:19

- The Holy Spirit abides within you.
  1 Corinthians 6:19-20; 2 Corinthians 6:16

- You have become a new person.
  2 Corinthians 5:17; John 3:3

- Your relationship with other people has changed.
  Matthew 6:12; Mark 11:25-26;
  1 John 3:11-24

- Be filled with the Spirit.
  Ephesians 5:18

What to do now!

- Pray daily.
  1 Thessalonians 5:17; Luke 18:1

- Read the Bible daily.
  Acts 17:11; Psalm 1:2

- Witness for Christ daily.
  Acts 1:8; Acts 5:42

- Confess Christ openly and be baptized.
  Matthew 10:32; Matthew 28:19-20; Acts 2:41

- Attend church where the Bible is preached and Christ is honored.
  Hebrews 10:25

- Keep Christ's commandments.
  John 14:15